The Miniature Costumier

REMOVABLE CLOTHING FOR DOLLS' HOUSE PEOPLE

CATRIONA HALL

SALLY MILNER
PUBLISHING

First published in 2004 by
Sally Milner Publishing Pty Ltd
PO Box 2104
Bowral NSW 2576
AUSTRALIA

© Catriona Hall 2004

Design: Ingrid Carlstrom
Editing: Anne Savage
Photography: Tim Connolly
Drawings: John D. Hall

Printed in China

National Library of Australia Cataloguing-in-Publication data:

Hall, Catriona.
The miniature costumier: removable clothing for dolls' house people.

ISBN 1 86351 329 9.

1. Doll clothes. 2. Doll clothes - Patterns.
3. Doll coverlets. 4. Doll coverlets - Patterns. I. Title.
(Series: Milner craft series).

745.5922

DISCLAIMER
The information in this instruction book is presented in good faith. However, no warranty
is given, nor results guaranteed, nor is freedom from any patent to be inferred. Since we
have no control over the use of the information contained in this book, the publisher
and the author disclaim liability for untoward results.

CONTENTS

INTRODUCTION 4

THE ILLUSION 9

FIGURES, MATERIALS AND EQUIPMENT 12

USING THE PATTERNS: techniques, stitches 20

JOANNA: formal day dress; evening bodice, evening skirt,
casual day dress, knickers, petticoat 35

SOPHIE: cloth doll, pinafore, blouse, knickers, angel costume 44

FRANCES: dress with embroidered collar, knickers, petticoat 52

DAVID: napkin, modern jacket, bib, pilchers, sun bonnet,
half petticoat, traditional gown, bonnet 58

ANNABEL: smocked dress, knickers 70

LACHLAN: underpants, sailor suit jacket, knee shorts 74

ISOBEL: striped top, jeans, pleated skirt, knickers 80

ARCHIE: underpants, shirt, trousers, jacket, tie 88

THE LINEN CUPBOARD: towels, table mats, napkins,
tea cloth, sheets and pillowcases 96

ACCESSORIES: shoes, hats 102

NOTES ON KNITTING: threads, knitting needles 105

BIBLIOGRAPHY 110

SUPPLIERS 111

ACKNOWLEDGEMENTS 112

INTRODUCTION

The ambition to do an unusual thing in a moderately remote place means facing limitations. These can be dealt with in several ways: abandon the unusual thing, modify the unusual thing, extend your own skill level to accomplish the unusual thing. The first option is no fun at all; the next two have much more potential.

Tasmania is a beautiful place, with a very pleasant life style. It is probably not the place you would expect to find the most esoteric craft supplies. That gives necessity every opportunity to be the mother of invention. Something about the environment propels artists towards excellence. When an artist sets out to produce something the raw materials have to be hunted for. The readily available things need to be carefully considered for uses beyond their original intention. Those less readily available need to be discovered through mail order or substitutions sought. There is an expectation that quality can be achieved despite the limitations. This is also true for miniatures. Throughout the world, in one-twelfth scale, furniture makers create brilliant furniture. With their full-sized hands and wood from real trees they make miniature drawers with perfect dovetails. Glass blowers make decanters with perfectly fitting ground stoppers using their full-sized hands and real glass. Silversmiths can make perfect teapots with hollow spouts and ebony handles, from sterling silver not cast, but formed by full-sized hands. Needle workers do breathtaking needlepoint. It has always seemed to me paradoxical that the figures inhabiting the spaces filled with these wonderful things are acceptable with clothing that is sewn onto, or worse, glued onto them.

The production of miniature clothing is no more difficult than any other miniature work. It does require thought and effort. It can also help to have some needle skills but if the will to succeed is there the skills can develop. Thought, effort and will are the vital ingredients. If you can sew clothes onto a figure you can sew them as easily off it, and make them come on and off into the bargain. It is not difficult. Bravery in the face of a needle and thread helps. The stitching required is fine but we are not talking yards and yards of fine sewing, just a few inches at most. The time invested is actually quite short while the satisfaction is enormous, a good cost/benefit ratio. It is stretching the comfort zone. I have average hands and slightly short sight, but these days any needle bigger than size 12 feels like a crowbar. A little practice will help you feel comfortable handling small pieces and small equipment. It can be done.

There are lots of great reasons for making lovely clothes for your figures. If you do spend time, love and effort making something gorgeous your figures are not going to spill chocolate ice cream down the front in the first five minutes, indulge in a growing spurt or argue about the colour and style, at least not loudly. Several advantages flow from the clothing being removable. The garments can be maintained and kept clean by laundering which extends their life. They are just more fun. The figures can participate in telling more than one story and there is always the potential of another story yet to come.

These figures are my own sculptures, each modelled individually in porcelain. I love making them and they look the way I want them. Every doll maker has different priorities. Some love glass eyes or separate fingers, some want to capture that single dramatic moment forever. I want to allow for change. Allowing for change gives the inhabitants of the dolls' house or setting an independent life. They remain our surrogates in that miniature world but because the ability for change exists, just having the clothes removable for instance, the characters have more options. They also have the opportunity for character development. Theirs can be an ongoing story, a fiction that lives in our imagination and gives that imagination a space in which to play. The concept is like that of a personal theatre where the scenes can change; the characters come and go as the story flows. Rumer Godden, in her books *The Dolls' House* (1948), *Miss Happiness and Miss Flower* (1960) and *Little Plum* (1963), now all in print again, expressed this very clearly. *Miss Happiness and Miss Flower* was the first book I read independently; it captured my heart then and has held it ever since. It is difficult for me now to tolerate figures unable to respond to the weather or celebrate important occasions. They need to have warm clothes in winter, dress up for glam evenings or pop on their PJs and snug up in bed with a book or a laptop. This dictates that their poses can change and their clothes can change.

My aim is to pass on to the next wave of doll makers, and to anyone who would like to make functional clothing for their dolls, the things I have spent years synthesising for myself. The accepted wisdom has been 'it is not practical to make removable clothes for dolls' house dolls' so people don't bother to try. With Rumer Godden firmly planted in my psyche, saying 'it is, it is', I did, I did. Success did not immediately bless my first efforts, it must be admitted, but as my husband remarked I was nothing if not perseverant; gradually things improved. Each incremental improvement contributed to a more satisfactory result. The objective is to make clothing that fits well, goes on and off easily, is well constructed and looks natural. It is probably not possible to reproduce every full-sized garment in miniature, and some do work better than others. Recognition of those limitations is important. One must acknowledge and embrace the limitations while simultaneously looking for ways they can be circumvented. This means everything is reconsidered—seams, edges, fabrics, patterns, stitches, trim—all reassessed for their ability to contribute to the end. The work still has to be beautiful.

Many of these techniques are derived from other forms of needlework. One was a direct transfer from English patchwork. This adaptation works, gives a good result and is neat inside and out (my grandmother may be watching). All would apply to dressmaking for larger dolls and make that a more satisfactory process as well. No starch or forming agents have been used. The garments are to be handled and changed and look as good as possible on the figure.

The characters in this collection, Frances, David, Lachlan, Isobel, Archie, Sophie, Annabel and Joanna, were chosen partly because they are my favourites and partly to give a good range of options: female/male, young/old. I use porcelain for the sculpture as, apart from enjoying the medium, it has a satisfying feel, allows fine detail and gives good longevity, given reasonable care. If you wish to make your own figures but don't wish to make the substantial investment porcelain requires there are several suitable modelling compounds available from good art and craft suppliers who can advise about their use.

Frances is the earliest sculpture in this collection. She is of comfortable proportions (not thin) and is quite short, comely and lively. Her presence in the moment is appealing. Her hands are modelled for sewing with a gold thimble.

David is a sleeping baby, that most virtuous of infants.

Sophie is my 3- or 4-year-old, a fun age for parents and the best age for Father Christmas. She has an angel outfit for the pageant.

Annabel is a serendipitous figure. Her dimples remind me of my friend Annabel who has the best dimples and the sunniest nature.

Lachlan, Isobel and Archie are three of the figures that formed part of my International Guild of Miniature Artisans Fellowship submission. Lachlan and Isobel are named for my children, having their second names. Archie is modelled from a photo of my grandfather. I wanted a firm man, and his jaw definitely fitted the purpose. Archie is also a family name.

Joanna is my favourite. Her three outfits are made from one pattern with the neckline adjusted. This demonstrates the way different interpretations can be achieved with small adjustments to a basic design.

Silk underwear

THE ILLUSION

The miniaturist's hobby is as varied as the people who pursue it. There are the collectors of antique houses and accoutrements, more modern toy collectors, those who make everything themselves, those who collect superb craftsman pieces and any combination of the above. For some, particularly the collectors of antique and older toys, perfect scale is irrelevant. There is a lot of appeal in the freedom and serendipitous quality of older houses—vitality despite the dust! Vitality is a nebulous thing, subjective, bound up in heart and feeling, easy to lose if one is too pedantic.

Dolls are excluded in many fine miniature collections but they do add desirable vitality and can be worthy citizens. In our full-scale world a doll is appreciated just as it is with no other load to carry. Once it is part of a collection where scale is strictly maintained the doll figure has a much more onerous role, in this case populating a place where enchantment is the result of illusion. Preservation of the illusion is the major issue for many collectors. And preservation of the illusion is the responsibility the doll must shoulder if it is to be accepted and included.

As these dolls are my own design I can make them just as I wish. My preference is not to see any joint, but as they need to change poses compromise is required. The problem with joints is that if they are too obvious they spoil the illusion, break the spell. Sitting and standing require hip and knee joints, and elbow and shoulder joints are also desirable. Joanna is to play the piano so she has to have hands that can rest on the keyboard. Her elbow joints allow some twist. A neck joint allows the figure to express a wider range of sentiments with one modelled expression but the joint still should not show. The wrists and ankles could have joints too but as visible joints greatly outweigh the advantages afforded by a variety of poses they are easy to forgo. The need to camouflage the joints affects aspects of the clothing design. Elbows and knees need to be covered—somehow; consider hem length/trousers/stockings. The neckline needs to cover the neck joint and if the neckline is low a choker necklace is needed, or a very hairy chest indeed for a gentleman.

Some things wreck the illusion immediately. I am not talking about strict accuracy this time but visual equivalence—what the eye will accept without question, allowing the illusion to thrive.

Multiple layers of seams can create conspicuous bulk, particularly at the neckline where they are most obvious. These layers have been designed out as much as possible for these projects. When designing your own things try to avoid having many seams falling together.

Please don't let zigzag machine stitching show. It is probably the greatest disillusionment of all.

Lace can be a very beautiful thing, delicate and refined. However, at this scale even the finest lace is visually equivalent to a rather coarse full-scale variety. This is frustrating as lace is inherently decorative and convenient to use—the Delilah of miniature sewing, it can betray the scale *instantly*. Usually something else, embroidery or hemstitching or nothing, is better. Mostly I avoid using lace and use other trim instead—except where very coarse lace would be acceptable and expected.
The angel outfit for Sophie could have had a lace edge and been visually equivalent to the heavy torchon or crochet work often seen on ecclesiastical vestments. If the garment is well made and fits properly, trim can be minimal. In my mind's eye is a memory of a photograph with the late Duchess of Windsor in a superb suit, totally plain except for the over-scaled self-rouleau-covered hook and eye closures—elegant but also witty. That designer earned their place in Heaven with that garment, whoever they were.

At the considerable risk of labouring the point, if you would not clutter a full-scale garment with details, they are even less desirable in 1:12 scale.

On the other hand …

Enrichment! Humans do love detail. It is wonderfully satisfying. In miniature it needs judicious expression; too much overloads and overwhelms. To my eye there is nothing worse than constipated frills of lace. The point of the lace is lost; delicacy and translucency and a coarse out-of-scale texture is added, doing no justice to lace or garment.

Enrichment can come in subtle ways. Consider the way light plays over the surface of clothing—colour, texture, reflectivity. These are the tools to work with when enrichment is the goal. Add the sheen of silk to a cotton garment in a belt or collar without changing colour or texture. Add a contrasting colour, a neutralised complementary for instance. Change the texture with smocking or embroidery in the same colour as the background. Subtlety is an underrated ally in this field and the eye does not always have to stop and register everything consciously for success to be achieved. Hems and edges are natural places for enrichment. Very finely executed spoke stitch at the hem is wonderfully satisfying but not obtrusive. A bound edge has two virtues—a neat finish and a line of interesting detail. This also applies to the embroidered buttonhole edge. They are there but accepted by the eye. Embroidery is a useful way of adding colour, texture and reflectivity. One motif, strategically placed—an edge celebrated or essential details like braid on a uniform—works best in carefully chosen embroidery. One can emulate Mary Delany in her famous court dress and create the embroidered fabric.

These are my opinions and prejudices. If you agree with them, good. If you disagree with them, good. Disagreement will help you crystallise what you like, what your opinions are, where your priorities lie. You will make your choices more clearly and with confidence.

FIGURES, MATERIALS AND EQUIPMENT

THE DOLL/FIGURE

Flexibility is the first thing to look for in the figures you select to dress. If they can move arms and legs it is easier to put clothes on and off. Hands are best modelled in a smooth pose without protruding digits, this reduces the risk of damage to the sleeve or finger. If fingers catch trouble is likely. This does not mean that hands cannot have an interesting pose or be well modelled, just that individual digits should not be exposed to the risk of breakage. Good proportions are also important. The normal human adult is seven of their own heads high, approximately. Children's heads are proportionally larger the younger they are. This is a subliminal signal to most of us. Without being aware of it we know the approximate age of an individual by their proportions. An over-large head makes an unconvincing adult, gives that dreaded 'something not quite right' feeling. When choosing kit dolls, look for those with hands without protruding fingers, good flexibility and good proportions. If making your own figures, the issues are still the same, naturally.

Every doll has its own personality, whether it is a commercial production or an individually sculptured one-off. If I say 'listen to what the doll tells you about itself', it looks rather silly on the page but in effect that is what I want to say. There may be doll makers who can set out to make a jolly publican and then make a jolly publican, but the last time I tried it was a clergyman who materialised. I could even hear him singing Wesleyan hymns 'lustily and with good courage'. His wife was to hand too, a formidable type who insisted on antique lace and a cameo. She got them despite all my reservations about lace. Another lady was a keen golfer with no interest in home life at all. Equipped with sensible shoes and a Fair Isle cardigan she was off. I may have produced them but something about them, the fanatical look in the eye or something else, dictated their personalities which then took over—a not unfamiliar experience. It usually means a more inspired, individual doll results. So do listen to what the figures tell you about colours, fabric or style. In the end you will have had an adventure and they will be more convincing.

FABRIC

There is a saying about quilters—'the one who dies with the most fabric, wins'. This is a risk for those dressing dolls' house people too. It seems to be one of the permutations of Murphy's Law that you can never find the fabric you need if you go out looking for it, but it will leap at you from the most unlikely place the day you leave your credit card at home. The tendency is to buy 'might come in handy' fabrics when they appear and it does seem to be the best way. I have a rather small collection of fabrics (part of a larger hoard, it must be admitted) which behave well in small-scale work. All-natural fibres, cotton, silk and linen, are the most useful. Fabrics which crease easily conform to the small body more satisfactorily. Lawn, batiste, voile, silk habutai and handkerchief linen are in constant use for all sorts of garments. They need to have fine warp and weft threads and be closely woven. Silk crepe tends to be too springy to sit well but very fine taffeta can be used where its stiffness is acceptable. I do wash taffeta very carefully, in small pieces, with wool wash and without creasing it. This does reduce some of the stiffening but is not recommended by the manufacturers, so it is done at one's own risk. Wash other washable fabrics before beginning. If the fabric is prone to shrinkage this will not affect your work. Washing can also remove some of the stiffening in many new fabrics and warns you if the colours are likely to run.

Lawn in a suitable colour, lined with silk habutai, makes a convincing overcoat. It is what the eye will accept, what looks right at this scale: a thicker fabric would not hang so well and could look odd. Silk habutai is one of the most useful fabrics. It is very fine and works well for lining or top fabric. There are a few fabrics produced for patchwork that can be used for heavier garments like this if chosen carefully; go for the finest possible weaves and natural fibres. It is always worth looking. Wool is a wonderful fibre but I haven't found any wool fabric suitable to use at this scale; so far, wool fabrics are far too springy and wilful. It would be a delight to discover one some day.

SILK RIBBON

Silk ribbon is useful for binding edges, making sashes and waist bands. It is also useful for facing hems when that last skerrick of favourite fabric is really too short. It takes dyes well and can be made into roses (Joanna's hat) and used in many other situations. The desirable feature of silk ribbon is its ability to scrunch up to nothing, like a magician's hankie (also silk), so very small perky bows are possible. When binding an edge and in use as a facing, its selvedge can be used and relied on. Silk ribbon is invaluable as it adds very little bulk wherever it is used.

THREAD

There is a traditional rule about thread: always use the same fibre as the fabric you are sewing. I would add, always use natural fibres—cotton, linen, silk. The reason for always using natural fibres is that fabrics made from natural fibres are more accommodating to small bodies than those with man-made fibres so man-made fabrics won't be used. Natural fibres have good longevity, given care. If you are putting effort into a work of artistic expression that you wish your great-grandchildren to take pride in, it is safer to use something we know can last that long.

Constructional sewing is best done with compatible thread. I do love to embroider cotton fabric with silk thread—the contrast of matt fabric and lustrous thread is satisfying—but that is not a stress-bearing situation. There is also, in constructional work, the time when cotton fabric is being lined with silk fabric. In that case either cotton or silk threads could be used and it comes down to the best colour match between thread and fabric. Matched thread colours and fabric colours give the advantage of camouflage for less than perfect stitches (should so unlikely a thing occur).

The thickness of thread is also relevant. Cotton thread for machine sewing comes in several thicknesses: 30, 50, 60, 80, with 30 being the thickest. The most useful in this work are 60 and 80; these weights are made by Mettler and Madeira Cotona (probably others too), usually available for 'heirloom' sewing and mostly in pastel colours. Gütermann make a range of pure cotton thread in a good range of colours in 50. It works better than 30. Silk threads come in similar thicknesses. I have recently been using YLI #100 pure silk thread. It has great colours and is a beautifully behaved thread: it does not tangle very often, does not wear out too quickly and is not too springy to settle in place. It is slippery, however, and can slip out of the needle. There are others. The quest for the best thread is part of the fun.

EQUIPMENT

Choosing the most suitable tools for hand sewing does make success more likely than failure. The right needle and thread will slip through finely woven fabrics with minimal resistance. The wrong one will make every stitch a battle and the resulting article will look like a battlefield because the stitches will not lie well.

Light

Good light always helps when doing fine work. As we age we need more light to work by. A good lamp illuminating the work and not shining in the eyes is often all that is needed, in addition to one's normal sewing or reading glasses, to see the stitches or the eye of that fine needle. Colours can be different when lit by daylight or by artificial light. It is instructive to check fabrics in both before committing oneself. I have one fabric which is buff coloured by daylight but a rather strange green under artificial light. This could be disconcerting if you were not aware of it beforehand.

Needles

The very best needles for these projects are good quality (usually English) No.12 sharps or betweens. If you really have trouble threading them, even in good light, try a large eye No.10 quilting needle. These have an eye more like a crewel needle, used for embroidery. I do have some No.12 crewel needles but they seem to cut the thread more often; another brand might be better but as I am very happy with the first option I have not pursued this. The larger the needle, the less easily it will slip through fine fabrics. Needle sizes start with low numbers for larger needles and progress to higher numbers for the finer ones.

Pins

Use fine pins. Those known as 'silk' pins are the finest as silk marks easily if coarse ones are used. It is best to use pins as briefly as possible: pins left in work for an extended period are more likely to leave a mark which could disfigure the article permanently. Sometimes one can pin outside the area to be sewn and still have security while basting is carried out.

Sewing Machine

Making these projects involves small pieces of fabric and short distances of stitching. They are the perfect size to disappear beneath the pressure foot of a sewing machine and give hours of fun untangling and rethreading. Hand stitching them is actually quicker and more relaxing.
It can be done in the company of your favourite music or your favourite people. If you must use a sewing machine, cut the pieces with generous margins then trim back to 3 mm (1/8 in) after the initial stitching is done. However, there are still going to be many tiny places where fingers can go with a needle but a sewing machine would have trouble reaching.

Sewing equipment

Thimbles

Habituating oneself to the use of a thimble is time well spent and repays the effort with time saved and eased performance. If you use one, you will have much greater power and speed, finer stitches, a whiter wash, *everything*. Try wearing it around the house for a while, just to get used to the feel of it on your finger. Eventually it feels natural and is easy to use. My favourite is a silver one my grandmother used but they are made in all sorts of materials. If you are allergic to a particular thimble or dislike it, there are others. The middle finger is usually the pushing finger and your thimble should fit it comfortably, without being too tight or too loose and likely to fall off.

Scissors

It is worth investing (I do mean that literally) in good embroidery
scissors; a small size for snipping threads and clipping inside curves of
seam allowances and a larger size for cutting out fabric and trimming.
Mine are 90 mm (3½ in) and 145 mm (5¾ in), made by WASA. I have had
less expensive pairs but they do not cut as consistently well and then
add insult by falling to pieces. They are not abused but are often in use.
Protect your good scissors tenaciously from vandals who filch them for
cutting paper and card. Keep less exalted pairs for this purpose.

Pencils

The pattern shape is transferred to the fabric using small pencil dots.
There needs to be enough dots to transfer the information clearly but as
few as possible. When using a very fine fabric like batiste, heavily marked
dots will show through to the right side, so make sure the dots are light
ones. Chose a medium lead (F or HB), keep it sharp and don't press too
hard. On dark fabrics a white or light coloured pencil does the same
thing. My favourite is a clutch pencil which uses a 2 mm lead: clutch
pencils with narrower leads seem to break more often.

Ironing sausages

I use ironing sausages in three sizes: 25 mm (1 in), 15 mm (½ in) and
7 mm (¼ in) diameter—or thereabouts—and all about 75 mm (3 in)
long. They are basically miniature tailor's hams and make ironing sleeves,
legs and bodices and so on possible without leaving nasty creases. They
are firmly stuffed with wool and covered in lawn. To make them, the lawn
is folded into a tube and the long side sewn firmly with 3 mm (⅛ mm)
seam allowances. Turn, gather one end closed, stuff firmly then gather
remaining end closed. For the 25 mm (1 in) diameter sausage you will
need to start with fabric that is 85 mm (3⅜ in) wide; the 15 mm (½ in)
diameter sausage will require a strip of fabric 47 mm (1⅞ in) wide and
the 7 mm (¼ in) diameter sausage will need a strip 28 mm (1⅛ in) wide.
These all include a 3 mm (⅛ in) seam allowance on each side.

Turning stick

The turning stick has been instituted to replace a use to which my scissors were most inappropriately put. I confess to using my scissors to turn things right side out in the olden days. They never did snip in the wrong place but it was always a risk so they have been replaced with a thick satay stick. Its point has been rounded with files and sandpaper so that it will not damage the fabric even if used enthusiastically and it is still pointy enough to ensure crisp corners. It is sensible to proceed slowly when turning. Turning really small things, like Sophie's cloth doll, needs to be approached with care—it can be done but any force needs to be judiciously applied. It does not hurt to stop and think about the problem for a moment, have a cup of tea and something to eat, then go back to it with better blood sugar levels. It is so satisfying when you have achieved it. The instructions for my solution to that challenge are in Sophie's chapter.

USING THE PATTERNS:

TECHNIQUES AND STITCHES

Practice will help achieve the most difficult challenge but it is sensible to acclimatise hands and eyes by starting on the simpler, more straightforward garments. There is nothing like doing something to teach you how it is done and to inform your next effort. Don't ever be disheartened if your first efforts don't meet your expectations: they will next time.

Read all the instructions through first to get a clear overview of the process before you begin.

Joanna's evening blouse and David's jacket are the easiest projects in this collection. David's long baby gown is much more challenging, needing tucks taken and precise embroidery. Archie's clothing is all demanding, more fitting, more fuss, although still fun of course. They are more satisfactorily achieved with the greater confidence gained from doing some simple things first.

Precision is necessary. Do be precise when cutting patterns, transferring patterns to fabric, cutting fabric and sewing. At this scale every millimetre does count. Trace the patterns as printed with tracing paper and a fine drawing pen (both available from any good stationer). Transfer all the information, cut with a generous margin, glue the pattern to thin card with a glue stick then cut accurately on the cutting line with a pair of sharp paper scissors.

Your doll's figure is not likely to be the same as those shown here. Most patterns will need testing and adjusting to get the best fit for the figure you are working on. Start with the given pattern, trace it onto a piece of fabric (fine lawn is most suitable) and cut out with a generous margin, at least 7 mm ($^1/_4$ in). Sew the seams with running stitch then fit this on your figure with the seams outside. Where are the adjustments needed? Too tight? Too loose? Too long or short? Mark those adjustments onto the fabric pattern with a marker or pen. Be prepared to redraw the pattern with its changes if necessary. Take all the stitching out and carefully iron flat without stretching it—using downward pressure is safest, rather than moving the iron along the creases. Trim the pattern to your new shape, allowing for seams, and glue this onto light card, then cut it accurately. It is now your pattern and you can confidently proceed with the garment.

This is a slower process than just using the patterns straight off, but it will give a far superior result and you will be so much more delighted with your effort that it is ten minutes well spent. A little more time spent on the preliminary stages and adequate attention given to the subsequent stages does pay off and does not take much more time—a lot less than getting things totally wrong and then starting again, although that is a useful experience too.

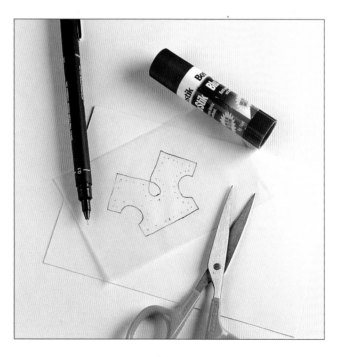

Pattern making equipment

DESIGN CONSIDERATIONS

One of the problems when designing removable clothing for 1:12 scale people is that fabric does not come in 1:12 scale. Choosing the fabric is important but designing the garment to avoid lumpiness and maintain the illusion is the most important priority. Shoulder seams, where lumpiness is most likely to occur, are also the most conspicuous spots when it does. Seams at the tops of sleeves do not present the same problem; they can give definition to the silhouette, rather more desirable than otherwise.

The choice of pattern in the fabric affects the choice of design for the garment. A plain or non-directional pattern can be used in any design but a fabric with an obvious directional pattern (like stripes) limits the design options. Stripes are interesting so don't abandon them, but do think about how they will flow and choose a design where they can work to advantage. Do avoid shoulder seams if at all possible. Isobel's striped top does this using a raglan design. Frances's striped dress of very fine silk does have a shoulder seam, but avoids it in the facing (also fine silk).

TRANSFERRING THE PATTERN TO FABRIC

Once you have a pattern it needs to be transferred to the fabric. This is achieved using small pencil dots. There needs to be enough of them to transfer the information clearly but as few as possible. When using a very fine fabric like batiste, heavily marked dots will show through to the right side so make sure the dots are light ones. Chose a medium lead (F or HB), keep it sharp and don't press too hard. On dark fabrics a white or light-coloured pencil does the same thing.

When using the patterns, cf means 'centre front' and cb means 'centre back'.

BASTING

Once the pattern is transferred and the fabric cut, pinning and basting may be needed, particularly where lining is employed. Use a fine needle and fine thread for basting because, although it is temporary, thick thread is still less comfortable to use and could leave marks in very fine fabrics. Basting gives control over the way the top fabric and its lining behave together, so it is worth the time it takes.

LININGS

Many of these patterns call for a lining. Patterns for these are not given as I baste then sew the top fabric to the lining before cutting the lining accurately along the cutting line. The lining is cut as a generous approximate shape to begin with. The result, when turned and pressed, is a shape with finished edges which can be joined using the overcast seam (fig. 5).

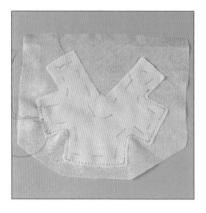

Making a lining

SEAMS AND SEAM ALLOWANCES

Seams require compromise between suppleness and strength. The most important aspect, strength, unobtrusiveness or flexibility, will dictate which type of seam to use. The simplest seam, running stitch (fig. 1) is the most supple and least bulky but the least strong, also the least durable or neat. The overcast seams (fig. 4 and fig. 5) are those I use most often. They are strong, fine and neat but not the most flexible. Run and fell seams (fig. 7) and French seams (fig. 6) I love for historic and sentimental reasons but usually they are too bulky and too stiff in this scale. The seam allowances shown on the patterns are those I habitually use, enough for strength but as small as possible to be unobtrusive. They work because the fabric is finely woven, the thread is fine and the stitches are small. Sometimes, when making a French seam, I overcast the first line of stitching, then do running stitch for the second in the usual way. This has the advantage of compressing and neatening the first line and controlling the tendency to fray, so that the whole can be very fine and neat. The disadvantage is that it is even stiffer than a normal French seam, but then they are already rather stiff and would not have been employed at all if stiffness was a problem. This is most often used on the centre back seam of skirts. To reduce the bulk in the hem, make a French seam from below the waist to the line where the hem will be stitched, then an open seam for the length inside the hem and hem as usual.

HEMS

A neatly sewn hem is part of any well-constructed garment. It will take different forms depending on where it is. There are times when an over-cast edge (fig. 4—worked on a single thickness of fabric) is the most suit-able. Closely and firmly worked with fine needle and thread it is neat and unobtrusive and can be invaluable for underwear and evening wear or for an edge that in full scale would normally be a selvedge (like the long sides of bed sheets). At the other extreme, a thicker fabric may need to have its raw edge overcast to neaten and stop fraying but then that edge should be folded up once only and hemmed. In most places plain hemming (fig. 3) is usually employed but that can be replaced by spoke stitch or hem stitching (fig. 11) if the article would benefit from that degree of elaboration. Hems can also be faced or bound with silk ribbon when there is insufficient fabric for a hem or it would improve the item. The other favourite technique for an especially delicate piece is the button-hole edge (fig. 9). This is not a quick fix to an edge problem but it can be a lovely one. It is definitely one that benefits from practice.

Spoke stitch is a very useful variation on hemstitching. On the right side the result is a decorative series of tiny holes and stitches echoing the hem line. It can be worked on bias grain and on curves. The stitching is done in exactly the same way hemstitching is performed (fig. 11) except that no threads are pulled at all. The little holes are the result of the needle and thread passing through the same hole three times and constricting the threads of the fabric. It is also possible to work a narrow needlepoint lace, using knot stitch (fig. 17), on an edge which has been hemmed or overcast previously. When worked using the finest silk or cotton thread, the scale is acceptable. This is not too arduous and can be delightful on a collar, baby things or undies.

Process of finishing the outer edge of a piece,
using buttonhole stitch, before cutting away fabric

Hems at the end of sleeves or trouser legs are very difficult to finish neatly inside and out, particularly if you sew the seams first. They are smaller than one's fingers which causes the difficulty. If you make the hem first the edge is ugly where the seam goes through the hem. To overcome this, the seam allowances inside the hems should be turned in before the hem is turned up and sewn. When the seam is sewn the folded edges are overcast firmly, giving a very neat finish with no nasty raw edges.

FASTENINGS

In my dreams there are functional, perfectly 1:12 scaled zip fasteners—if only! This is the place limitations do get rather frustrating and a little subterfuge is needed. Zips can be implied and the actual fastening performed by beads and embroidered loops (fig. 10), or beads and buttonholes or, very occasionally, buttons. Functional 1:12 scale buttons are not common things although there are a few available. I mostly use #13 glass beads (Mill Hill petites) in colours to match the fabric and worked buttonhole loops. These are unobtrusive in use but relatively comfortable for adult hands to operate. If #13 is truly too small, even after lots of trying, use a slightly larger bead. The fastening uses a levering action. The loop has to be just the right size. Too tight won't fit over the bead and too large won't stay closed. This is something best learned with experience; doing them a few times will help develop the judgement needed to get them right—most of the time.

STITCHES

This section includes the stitches which are the most useful and most commonly used in all these projects. Many of them will be familiar. If the method shown is different to the one you know, do whichever you prefer. There are several ways of doing many stitches and processes and the methods given here are explanatory, not definitive. They are meant to be a place to start. Small stitches are not just for appearance. A given length of stitching will be subject in wear to a certain amount of stress. If that stress is shared by a larger number of stitches each stitch has less stress to bear individually and is that much less likely to break or fail. Smaller stitches increase the active life of the article.

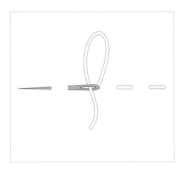

Fig. 1 *Running stitch*

This is the most basic stitch used anywhere. Start with two or three stitches taken in the same place until the thread is securely anchored. Do avoid knots; they are most unreliable and will make a lump in your work which will wear a hole over time. Practice making the stitches as small as possible.

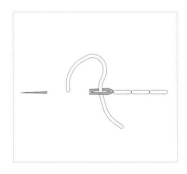

Fig. 2 *Backstitch*

Backstitch is useful for several reasons; it has some built in stretch, is visually continuous and is also strong.

Fig. 3 Hemming

This is an inconspicuous finish, therefore wonderful in miniature work, when made with the fewest threads possible picked up.

Fig. 4 Overcast seam 1

This gives a very thin, firm seam. When worked over a single thickness of fabric it makes a firm inconspicuous edge or restrains a fabric from fraying.

Fig. 5 Overcast seam 2

This has a separate drawing as it is worked over previously finished edges (lined or basted) and is worked closely on the very edge of the folds. It is very neat and strong and internally the seam allowances are distributed evenly so any unwanted bulk is distributed less conspicuously.

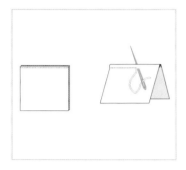

Fig. 6 French seam

This is a very neat seam but not very flexible in this scale, so is mostly used on the back of skirts. Start the seam on the right side of the work, trim any loose threads, then turn right side in and sew the second line of stitches as closely as possible to the first.

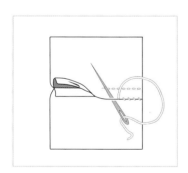

Fig. 7 Run and fell seam

This seam was traditionally used for undergarments. It is also a very neatly finished seam.

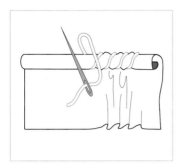

Fig. 8 *Whipped gathers*

This is a very useful technique for miniature-scale work as it neatens and gathers at the same time. I find it particularly good for very small garments for babies and small children. It is rather pretty when worked evenly too.

Fig. 9 *Buttonhole stitch*

Buttonhole stitch gives a fine and decorative edge in many different situations. It can be a feature or unobtrusive.

Fig. 10 *Buttonhole loop*

In most situations a cut buttonhole is too clumsy for garments in this scale and the buttonhole loop is neat and inconspicuous. It is reasonably easy for full-sized hands to manipulate with practice.

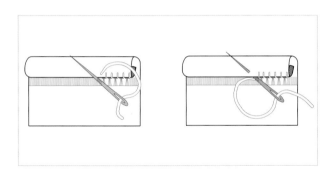

Fig. 11 *Hemstitching*

There are several versions of hemstitching; this is the one I use. It must be worked on a straight edge as several threads are pulled out parallel to the hem. It is a subtle stitch and while not a quick stitch is very satisfying to work and look at. Spoke stitch is worked in exactly the same way but no threads are pulled so it is possible to work on a bias or curved edge. This has the added advantage from our point of view of being a finer stitch when completed.

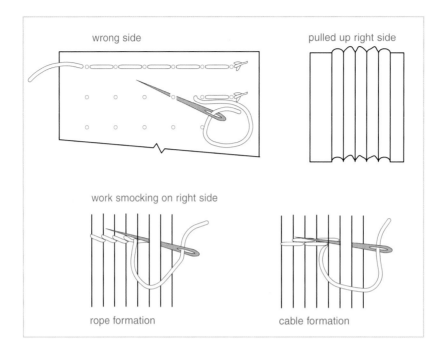

Fig. 12 *Smocking*

The most basic stitches are the best to use in small work because the stitches themselves do not take much space and there can be enough of them to look convincing. The gathering threads create vertical tubes when they are pulled and tied off. The embroidery is worked onto the tubes on the right side of the garment.

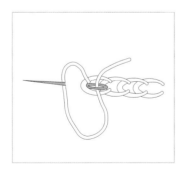

Fig. 13 *Chain stitch*

Chain stitch is very good value. It gives a strong line with most of the thread on the surface. It forms the basis of many other stitches, some of which follow.

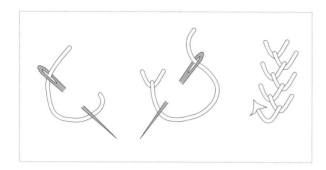

Fig. 14 *Feather stitch*

There is something very satisfying about feather stitch; it seems to have a swinging rhythm. One of the descendants of chain stitch.

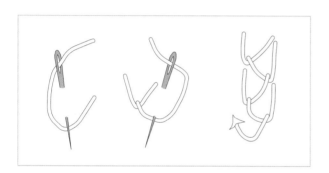

Fig. 15 *Closed feather stitch or double chain stitch*

This is a stitch which can be useful as a substitute for lace insertion. It gives interest to the surface in the way insertion does in a larger scale but is much smaller and so more satisfactory at 1:12.

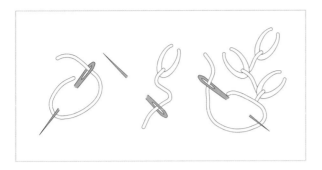

Fig. 16 *Chained feather stitch*

Like the preceding stitch this is a very pretty stitch in miniature and a good replacement for lace.

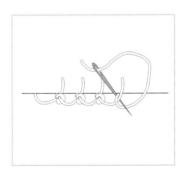

Fig. 17 *Knot stitch*

Another lace alternative; it is a needlelace, in fact. This is a variation on blanket stitch or buttonhole stitch: the trick is to only tighten the knot when the thread is in place. If a scalloped edge is desired this can be combined with the simpler stitch—three knot stitches, then one blanket stitch, and so on. I prefer to work it on a finished edge, but if a raw edge has to be dealt with, overcast it first using small, firm stitches but not distorting the edge.

JOANNA

Joanna has three outfits. The holly print dress, cream dress and an evening outfit. The cream dress gives the basic procedure. The holly print dress uses one of my all time favourite Liberty prints. Not really a holly leaf at all, more like an oak leaf, but in this colour it reminds me of Dickensian Christmases, 'bah humbug', Tiny Tim and all the rest of it, so I always call it the holly print. It is a great scale for 1:12 miniature garments and the weave is most satisfactorily fine. This dress has a Peter Pan collar of plain cream lawn edged in cherry-coloured 4 mm (5/32 in) silk ribbon which also finishes the sleeves. The cherry does reinforce the Dickensian atmosphere. Actually the complementary colours do no harm.

Joanna in her holly print dress

JOANNA'S MEASUREMENTS

Height: 140 mm (5^{1}/$_{2}$ in)

Bust: 75 mm (3 in)

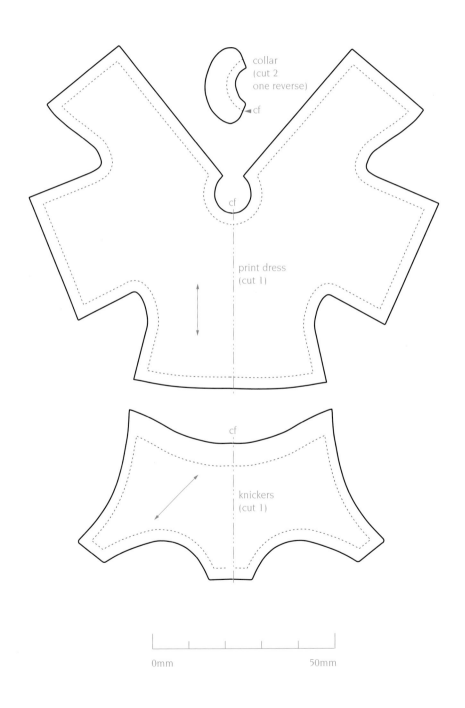

collar
(cut 2
one reverse)

◄ cf

cf

print dress
(cut 1)

cf

knickers
(cut 1)

0mm   50mm

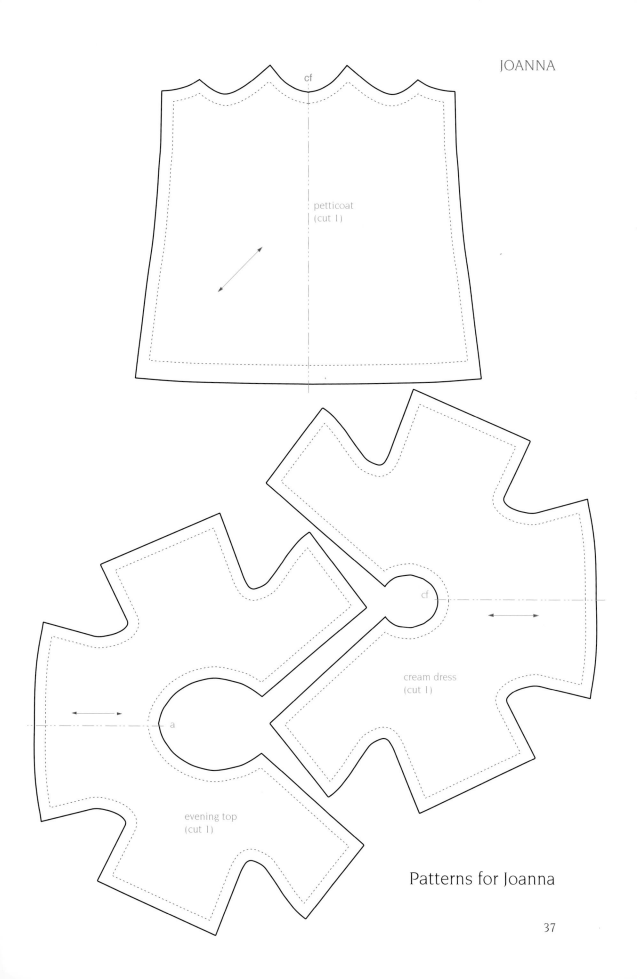

cf

petticoat
(cut 1)

cream dress
(cut 1)

cf

a

evening top
(cut 1)

Patterns for Joanna

The cream dress is made by lowering the neckline a little and using a delicate fabric, this time a very fine Swiss batiste. The pattern gives a garment for the Spring Racing Carnival with the race that stops a nation, or a summer wedding, perhaps a garden party. The accessories confirm the impression that a bubbling cuvée of some variety is likely to be involved.

For evening, by lowering the neckline again and making in soft silk, the same bodice pattern gives a top that can be gently or seriously formal. Here teamed with a stiff taffeta skirt and a belt of antique beads, it is a rather romantic outfit. The belt could also be made with couched gold thread or other embroidery, something to give an exotic touch.

FORMAL DAY DRESS

You will need
  Batiste, silk habutai for lining, 2 beads, silk ribbon for sash

Method
  • Trace bodice pattern onto batiste with small dots. Place centre front on the straight of the grain. Cut accurately.
  • Cut a rectangle of batiste for the skirt 63 x 200 mm (2½ x 8 in) on the straight of the grain (pattern not given for this).
  • Place bodice right side down onto silk lining, pin and baste so that the batiste
  and lining lie smoothly together. Cut bodice lining with a generous seam allowance, 15 mm (½ in), but do not trim accurately yet.
  • Sew around bodice, 3 mm (⅛ in) in from cutting line, using small firm running stitches and a few backstitches at corners and at changes of direction. Leave the waist edges open; these will be used for turning the bodice right side out later.
  • Remove basting threads, trim both fabrics to cutting line. Clip inside curves and turn right side out, making sure all corners are crisp. Iron flat.

- Fold bodice along shoulder line, right side in and overcast underarm seams (fig. 5). Open and flatten these, turn bodice right side out and use ironing sausages to press.
- Overlap the two sides of the back opening and stitch together at waist edge.
- Check fit on figure and adjust as needed.
- Make centre back seam in skirt (overcasting or a French seam is suitable here depending on the fabric.)
- Check length with bodice in place (allow for waist seam), then double fold and sew hem.
- Mark centre front in the seam allowance of skirt. Divide the skirt in halves again to find the points of the skirt which match the side seams of the bodice; mark these in the seam allowance. Pin these in place and distribute the extra fullness in two soft pleats (not ironed) either side of centre front and centre back.
- Sew skirt to bodice: baste first, then running stitch, trim and overcast to restrain fraying.
- Turn right side out and press waist seam (upwards), hover iron over pleats but do not press firmly.
- Sew 2 beads and embroidered loops at the back of bodice to close.
- Trim with 7 mm (¹/₄ in) silk ribbon sash at waistline.

EVENING BODICE

Joanna's evening bodice is made in soft fine silk, using the same procedure for the bodice as given for the cream dress except that it is sewn all around, including the waistline, leaving a small opening for turning under one arm, which is closed as the underarm seam is overcast. It may benefit from more beads and embroidered loops at centre back to fasten it.

Joanna in evening ensemble

EVENING SKIRT

The evening skirt is a rectangle of silk taffeta (a pattern for this is not given). It has a centre back seam and a placket opening.

You will need
  Silk taffeta, silk ribbon, bead

Method
  • Cut the taffeta on the straight of the grain, 2800 x 90 mm (11 x 3½ in).
  • Sew the centre back seam using a French seam, and leaving an opening for the placket 25 mm (1 in) below the waistline.

• Hem the placket with narrow hems turned from the seam allowance.

• Check the length on your figure before turning up the hem and hemming with very tiny stitches.

• Softly pleat the waist edge to fit waist, baste or overcast as you go, then stitch to a 7 mm (^{1}/4 in) silk ribbon waist band of the appropriate length.

• Turn in short ends, turn selvedge over raw edges, then hem in place.

• Fasten with a bead and embroidered loop on the waist band.

Hover iron to set but not crease pleats into place.

CASUAL DAY DRESS

The major difference between this casual print dress and Joanna's cream dress is the addition of the Peter Pan collar. As there is a centre back opening the collar is in two pieces. Remember to reverse the pattern when tracing the second piece of the collar. To eliminate extra layers at the neckline there is only one thickness of fabric for the collar, but then the raw edge has to be dealt with. This can either be embroidered with a buttonhole edge (fig. 9), bound with silk ribbon or have a fine needlepoint lace edge worked round it (fig. 17). If you wish to try the lace edge, cut the collar outline accurately but leave the neck edge uncut until the lace is complete to give you something to hold on to. Overcast the edge to be embroidered closely and firmly without distorting the shape. Work the knot stitch shown in fig. 17. It is sensible to try the technique out on a piece of scrap fabric until you are confident with it. The edge of the collar is worked (and ironed if necessary) before it is trimmed and basted into place, right side up on the right side of the cut out bodice. The bodice is then placed right side down on the silk lining where it is basted carefully.

The rest of the instructions are the same as for the cream dress. Press the collar in place once the bodice is lined and before the underarm seams are overcast.

Joanna wearing afternoon frock

KNICKERS

YOU WILL NEED
Silk habutai or lawn, 200 mm (8 in) shirring elastic

METHOD
• Cut pattern from either silk or lawn with the grain on the bias.
• Fold in ends of waist hem and baste in place (small stitches).
• Fold down and press double fold of waist hem.
• Place elastic, folded in half, inside fold of hem, loop peeping out one end and tails out the other.
• Hem waist hem over elastic but don't catch the elastic.
• Fold and hem leg edges of knickers with tiny hems.

- Turn right side in and overcast or run and fell centre back seam.
- Draw up elastic to fit waist and knot free ends through loop. Trim tails and tuck into waist hem.
- Overcast seam between legs firmly. Turn right side out and press.

PETTICOAT

YOU WILL NEED

Silk habutai or lawn, 3 mm (1/8 in) silk ribbon

METHOD

- Cut petticoat pattern on the bias in either silk or lawn.
- Cut another bias strip 100 x 38 mm (4 x 1 1/2 in) in the same fabric to make a facing for the top section of the petticoat.
- Baste petticoat to facing, right sides together.
- Sew on the sewing line where the facing is, partway down back seam on each side and the curved top.
- Trim. Clip inside curves and turn right side out and press.
- If the petticoat will slip over the body of your figure without a back opening overcast faced edges and overcast or run and fell the rest of centre back seam. If an opening is needed to get the petticoat on, leave 20 mm (3/4 in) of the faced back seam open, make the rest of the back seam as above and close with a bead and embroidered loop closure.
- Measure and attach 3 mm (1/8 in) silk ribbon straps to the high points on the top of the petticoat body.
- Check length and hem, or bind the hem with silk ribbon.

SOPHIE

Three-year-old girls are great fun to dress. Before they go to school and fall prey to the dreaded peer group pressure, Mum is wonderful and whatever she says is right. Nostalgia? Absolutely! This is a simple pinafore, straightforward to make, easy to launder and put on and take off. It is shown over a blouse with puffed sleeves but could be worn over a cardigan or jumper in cold weather. The other pattern given for Sophie is a basic nightgown pattern, simple, quick and effective. It is the type known as an 'angel' design when my daughter was small. It can be decorated by smocking the neck with the simplest of smocking stitches. The most basic ones are the best to use in small work as the stitches themselves do not take much space and there can be enough of them to look convincing. The top of the gown is nearly straight but needs to be drawn into a tight curve, almost three-quarters of a circle.

The vertical tucks are formed by making horizontal lines of tiny stitches and pulling these up (see fig. 12). The gathering thread on the neck edge is pulled more tightly so that the tucks lie more tightly there and are wider apart towards the shoulder. The tucks radiate. The stitching is done that way too. The neck edge is bound with silk ribbon before the original gathering threads are removed. The smocking can be omitted and the neck simply gathered and bound with the ribbon as previously. It is still nice to elaborate the bottom hem and sleeves with hemstitching or spoke stitch.

CLOTH DOLL

This is one time when it is easier to cut and trace the pattern on what will be the sewing line and add the seam allowances afterwards.

You will need

Fine fabric for body, lawn face fabric, embroidery threads, silk ribbon

Method

- Place the card pattern on a double square of fabric, allowing 7 mm ($1/4$ in) margin around the pattern. The fabric should be on the bias.
- Sew on the drawn line with very small stitches, using backstitches where the stitching changes direction, and leave a gap for turning at the top of the head, 7 mm ($1/4$ in) wide.
- Trim the seam allowance to 3 mm ($1/8$ in) and clip inside curves to stitching line without cutting the stitches.
- Turn right side out. This is not easy. The best way is to securely attach a silk thread to the seam allowance at the end of each limb, slip the needle (eye end if you can) into the body and exit through the turning gap, *without catching any fabric on the way*. Silk thread is stronger and is less likely to break when pulled. Do this to both arms and legs then gently pull all through together, pushing with the turning stick as well. Breathe a sigh of relief and pat self on back when achieved.
- Stuff with small tufts of stuffing pushed into place with turning stick.
- Gather edges of turning gap and slip stitch closed very firmly.
- Cut face pattern from face fabric adding seam allowance, gather around edge and tuck in raw edges, then place in position on head and hem around face with tiny stitches.
- Embroider basic eyes and mouth and a few strokes for hair.
- Tie ribbon round neck firmly to trim and define neck.

SOPHIE'S MEASUREMENTS

Height: 85 mm (3^{1}/4 in)

Chest: 50 mm (2^{1}i4 in)

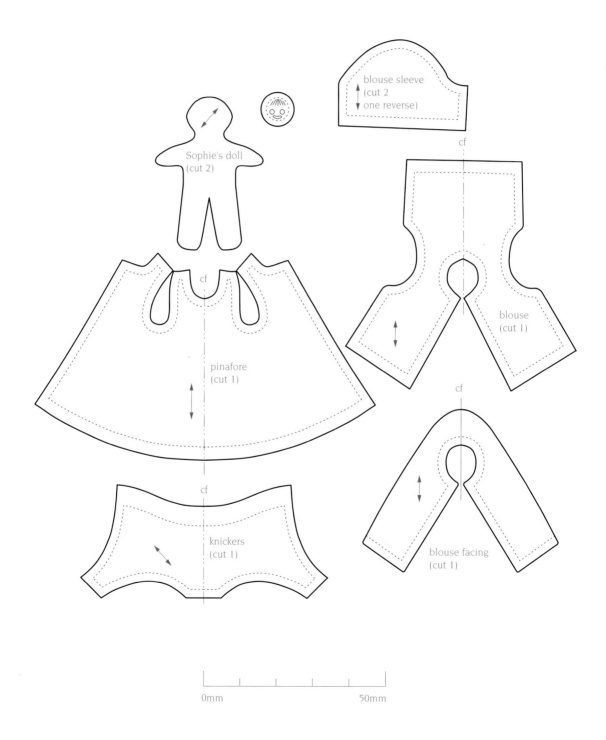

Sophie's doll
(cut 2)

blouse sleeve
(cut 2
one reverse)

cf

blouse
(cut 1)

cf

blouse facing
(cut 1)

pinafore
(cut 1)

cf

knickers
(cut 1)

cf

0mm   50mm

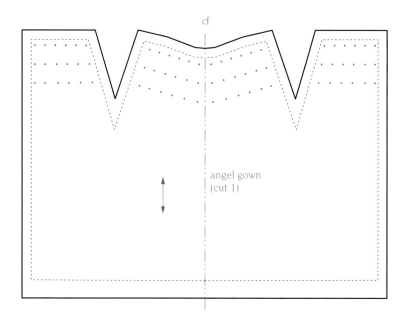

cf

angel gown
(cut 1)

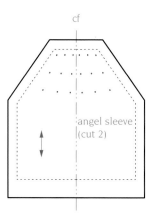

cf

angel sleeve
(cut 2)

Patterns for Sophie

PINAFORE

You will need
  Lawn, silk habutai for lining, bead

Method
  • Trace and cut pattern for pinafore on the lawn. Cut lining with a generous margin.
  • Place pinafore right side down on lining and pin and baste so that they lie smoothly together.
  • Sew along the sewing line through both thicknesses but leave a turning gap in the lower back seam.
  • Trim seam allowances to 3 mm ($^1/_8$ in), clip inside curves.
  • Turn right side out, using turning stick to make all corners crisp. Iron.
  • Fold right side in and overcast centre back seam to 25 mm (1 in) below neckline, closing turning gap in passing. Overcast shoulder seams.
  • Attach bead and work embroidered loop at back of neck to close.

BLOUSE

Sophie's blouse has puffed sleeves and is bound at the neck and sleeves with silk ribbon. It opens down the back and is partly faced with silk habutai.

You will need
  Lawn, silk habutai, 4 mm ($^5/_{32}$ in) silk ribbon, bead

Method
  • Trace and cut body and sleeves from lawn, reversing the sleeve pattern to give right and left sleeves. Trace and cut facing.
  • Pin and baste facing to body, right sides together. Sew centre back seams and hems. • Turn and press.

• Bind neck with silk ribbon, tuck short ends of ribbon inside binding and hem firmly in place.
• Gather bottom edge of each sleeve to fit over hand and arm when closed.
• Use ribbon to bind bottom of sleeves, tuck in short ends of ribbon, hem firmly.
• Gather top edge of sleeve to fit armhole of body and sew to body with running stitch, then overcast raw edges. The scooped side of the sleeve faces front.
• Turn right side out, take up and hem remaining length of hem. Press.
• Turn right side in and overcast underarm and sleeve seams.
• Attach bead and work embroidered loop at back of neck to close.

Sophie wearing pinafore and blouse and carrying her cloth doll

KNICKERS

You will need
Silk habutai or lawn, 150 mm (6 in) shirring elastic

METHOD
- Trace and cut pattern from either silk or lawn with the grain on the bias.
- Fold in ends of waist hem and baste in place (small stitches).
- Fold down and press double fold of waist hem.
- Place elastic, folded in half, inside fold of hem, loop peeping out one end and tails out the other.
- Hem waist hem over elastic but don't catch the elastic.
- Fold and hem leg edges of knickers with tiny hems.
- Turn right side in and overcast or run and fell centre back seam.
- Draw up elastic to fit waist and knot free ends through loop. Trim tails and tuck into waist hem.
- Overcast seam between legs firmly. Turn right side out and press.

Sophie in her angel outfit beside the Christmas tree

ANGEL COSTUME

The angel costume can be a nightgown if you wish but is shown as an angel outfit for Christmas festivities.

You will need
  Lawn or batiste, 4 mm ($^5/_{32}$ in) silk ribbon 150 mm (6 in) long, wings

Method
  First decide whether you are going to try the smocking or not. You will need 3 rows of dots for smocking and these are probably easier to mark before you start cutting and sewing. Although they radiate the number of vertical tubes stays the same, so there are the same number of dots in each row. On the front of the gown and on the sleeves the dots will need to curve to follow the shape but there will still be the same number of dots. If you are using fine lawn or batiste you should be able to trace the smocking dots off the pattern through the fabric. If not, use some dressmaking carbon paper to mark them.

  • Trace and cut pattern pieces.
  • Hem centre back hems with very narrow plain hems and take up bottom hem with spoke stitch or hem stitching. Press.
  • Turn in short ends of sleeve hems, turn up and hem. Work these in spoke stitch or hem stitching if you wish.
  • Overcast underarm seams on both sleeves and turn right side out.
  • Sew sleeves into armholes using overcasting.
  • Work gathering threads for smocking if using. Pull these into the three-quarter circle and knot off at the back.
  • Work smocking (fig. 12) as two rows of rope formation and two of cable formation, working from the neck out and easing the tension as you work outwards.
  • Gather neck edge to fit neck.
  • Stitch ribbon over neck edge, leaving generous tails on either side to tie garment closed. Remove gathering threads from smocking.
  • Stitch wings onto the back of the gown.

FRANCES

Frances takes the role of grandmother. She is a very responsive and sociable character, as were mine. One of them took clothes very seriously and I suspect Frances may do so too. Her dress is one of the more difficult garments in this book because to use the fine striped silk the shoulder seam is needed to ensure the stripes run correctly all round the dress. It has set in sleeves for the same reason, and embroidered collar and cuffs. The neck and collar are faced with a single facing which keeps the number of layers in that critical area within reason, but is rather tricky to achieve as this area cannot be worked on flat. It is probably sensible not to attempt this garment first.

Frances in her striped frock

DRESS WITH EMBROIDERED COLLAR

YOU WILL NEED

Silk or lawn for dress, silk habutai or plain lawn or batiste for collar, cuffs and belt, silk habutai for lining, 5 beads or buttons

METHOD

• Trace patterns for collar, cuffs and belt on chosen fabric, trace dress on to dress fabric, reverse the sleeve pattern to give right and left sleeves, and trace facing on silk habutai.

• Cut out dress but don't cut slit for front pleat yet. Cut facing and belt, but don't cut collar and cuffs until after the embroidery is complete.

• Work edge of collar and cuffs by first making a line of fine running stitches along the dots of the edge to be embroidered. The dots are marked on the wrong side so this line of running stitch gives the line to embroider on the right side. Pass the needle to the right side and work buttonhole stitch closely over the running stitch. Cut closely along the edge of the buttonhole stitch with sharp scissors but *don't* cut the stitching, please. Press, turn and cut out the rest of the collar and cuffs along the dotted lines.

• Sew shoulder seams with running stitch and press open.

• Baste collar right side up in place on the right side of the dress; it should fall short of the centre back on both sides.

• Place facing over the collar and bodice, carefully pin and baste together, through all layers.

• Sew centre back and neckline, again through all layers.

• Trim seam allowances, baste facing in place. Test fit on your figure.

• Check length of sleeves and adjust. Place cuff over sleeve, right side of cuff to wrong side of sleeve. This is a reverse facing so it is sewn inside then turned outside and pressed. Sew bottom of sleeve and up each side seam 3 mm ($^1/_8$ in). Turn cuff to the right side and press.

• Ease top of sleeve with fine gathering stitches and stitch into arm-hole, using running stitch then overcasting to restrain fraying, and treating dress and lining as one fabric.

• Overcast underarm seams.

FRANCES'S MEASUREMENTS

Height: 135 mm (5$\frac{1}{4}$ in)

Bust: 80 mm (3$\frac{1}{4}$ in)

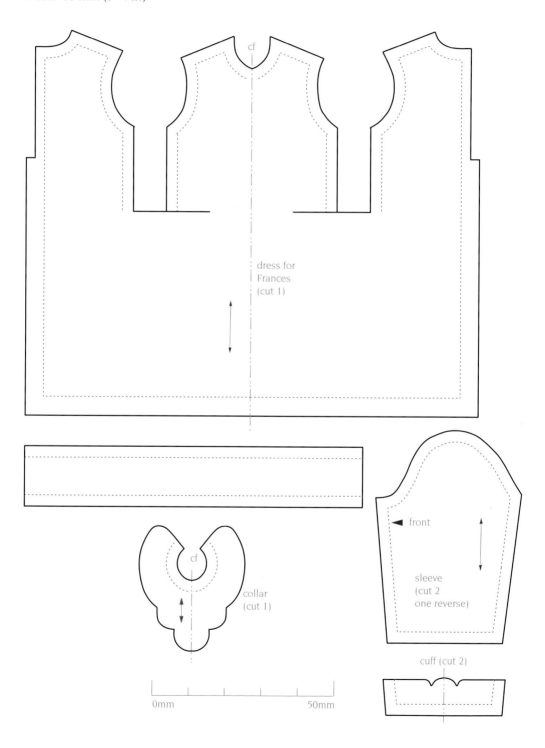

cf

dress for
Frances
(cut 1)

collar
(cut 1)

cf

front

sleeve
(cut 2
one reverse)

cuff (cut 2)

0mm   50mm

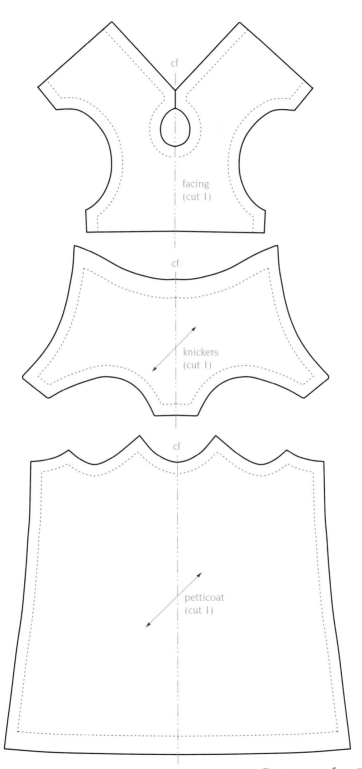

facing
(cut 1)

knickers
(cut 1)

petticoat
(cut 1)

Patterns for Frances

• At the point where the underarm seam stops, clip as shown on pattern towards the front of the dress. This will make an inverted pleat about 10 mm (³/₈ in) in from the side seam on each side. Push excess fabric towards centre front.

• Stitch pleats in place and close slit with edge-to-edge stitches like lacing so that everything lies flat. This will be covered by the belt.

• Sew back seam and make a pleat below back facing, stitch at hip level in line with front pleats.

• Press with the ironing sausages.

• Check hem length and hem, press.

• Sew bead and work embroidered loop at back of neck to close.

• Make the belt by folding the strip in half and making a long tube by sewing down the long side with running stitch. Turn right side out (sew a thread to one end firmly then push needle through the tube, eye end first, and use the thread to pull the belt right side out). Press flat, measure correct length on your figure, work buttonhole stitch over one end, trim length and work buttonhole stitch over second end, stitch in place over top of pleats and trim with a button or bead.

KNICKERS

YOU WILL NEED
Silk habutai or lawn, 200 mm (8 in) shirring elastic

METHOD
• Trace and cut pattern from either silk or lawn with the grain on the bias.

• Fold in ends of waist hem and baste in place (small stitches).

•Fold down and press double fold of waist hem.

• Place elastic, folded in half, inside fold of hem, loop peeping out one end and tails out the other.

• Hem waist hem over elastic but don't catch the elastic.

• Fold and hem leg edges of knickers with tiny hems.

• Turn right side in and overcast or run and fell centre back seam.

- Draw up elastic to fit waist and knot free ends through loop. Trim tails and tuck into waist hem.
- Overcast seam between legs firmly. Turn right side out and press.

PETTICOAT

You will need
Silk habutai or lawn, 3 mm (¹/₈ in) silk ribbon

Method
- Trace and cut petticoat pattern on the bias in either silk or lawn.
- Cut another bias strip 100 x 38 mm (4 x 1¹/₂ in) in the same fabric to make a facing for the top section of the petticoat.
- Baste petticoat to facing, right sides together.
- Sew on the sewing line where the facing is, partway down back seam on each side and the curved top.
- Trim. Clip inside curves and turn right side out and press.
- If the petticoat will slip over the body of your figure without a back opening overcast faced edges and overcast or run and fell the rest of centre back seam. If an opening is needed to get the petticoat, on leave 20 mm (³/₄ in) of the faced back seam open, make the rest of the back seam as above and close with a bead and embroidered loop closure.
- Measure and attach 3 mm (¹/₈ in) silk ribbon straps to the high points on the top of the petticoat body.
- Check length and hem, or bind the hem with silk ribbon.

DAVID

Baby David has a traditional gown with embroidery and tucks, with a matching bonnet and half petticoat, but he also has a set of more contemporary items. The traditional gown is a late nineteenth century design with an elaborately tucked and embroidered front panel which resembles an apron. The bonnet is made to match it. My father wore a gown very like this in the early 1900s. His was made of cream silk and although I still have it, it is no longer in a functional condition (as a five-year-old I put it on our corgi, who completely failed to be transformed into a Beatrix Potter character). The gown is satisfying to make but it is a demanding design with extra measuring and sewing. It could be made in silk habutai, Swiss batiste or fine lawn, but bear in mind that cotton fabrics are easier to handle than silk. You can decide how elaborate to make the embroidery: the bands on the front could be chain stitch (fig. 13), feather stitch (fig. 14), closed feather stitch (fig. 15) or chained feather stitch (fig. 16), or you could draw threads and work hemstitching on each side (fig 11). Don't be in a hurry when working on it and do try some of the simpler things first.

David wearing his jacket, pilchers and sun bonnet

NAPKIN

Cut a 38 mm (1 $\frac{1}{2}$ in) square of cream lawn (pattern not shown), fold in half diagonally to make a triangle with the fold on the longest side. Sew the two short sides with running stitch, leaving a small gap for turning. Trim, turn right side out and press. Slip stitch gap closed, fit on baby and stitch where you would pin. It will still come off.

DAVID'S MEASUREMENTS
Height: 55 mm (2^{1}/4 in)

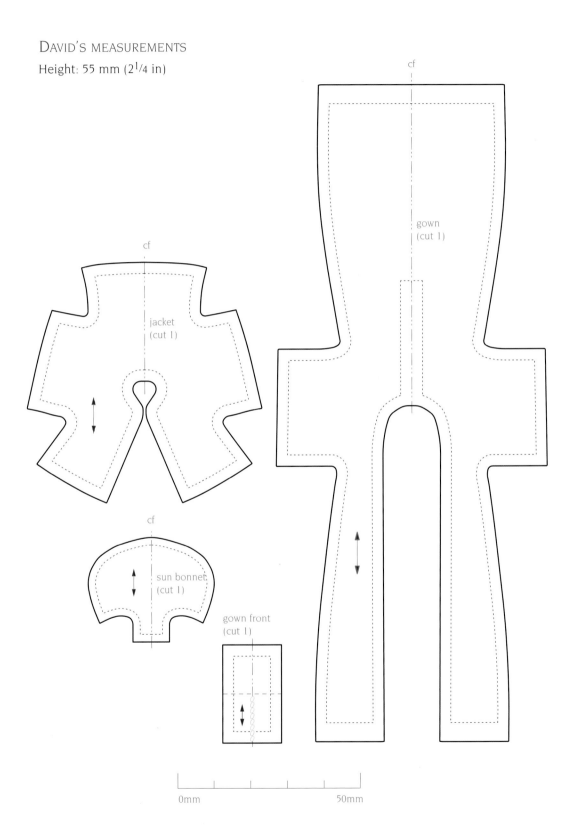

cf

gown
(cut 1)

cf

jacket
(cut 1)

cf

sun bonnet
(cut 1)

gown front
(cut 1)

0mm

50mm

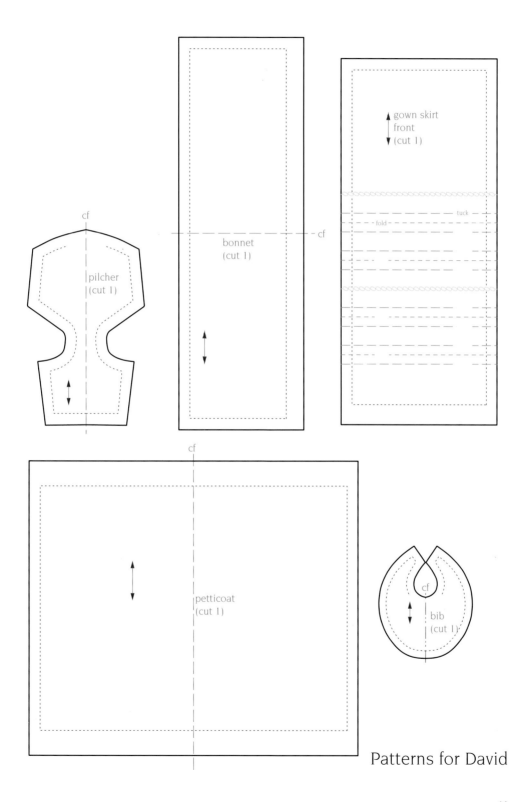

pilcher
(cut 1)

bonnet
(cut 1)

gown skirt
front
(cut 1)

tuck

fold

petticoat
(cut 1)

bib
(cut 1)

Patterns for David

MODERN JACKET

YOU WILL NEED
Printed or plain lawn, silk habutai for lining, bead

METHOD
• Trace and cut jacket pattern with centre back on the straight of grain. Cut lining with a generous allowance of 15 mm ($^1/_2$ in). Do not trim accurately yet.
• Place jacket right side down onto silk lining, pin and baste so that the fabric and lining lie smoothly together.
• Sew around jacket on sewing line with small running stitches, using backstitch at the corners and changes in direction. Leave a small gap for turning in back underarm seam.
• Remove basting threads, trim both fabrics to cutting line. Clip inside curves, turn right side out, making sure all corners are crisp. Press.
• Fold jacket along shoulder line, right side in and overcast underarm seams, closing turning gap in passing.
• Turn right side out, sew bead and embroider loop to close.

BIB

YOU WILL NEED
Printed or plain lawn, silk habutai for lining, bead

METHOD
• Trace bib pattern on straight of grain and cut, but don't cut neckline.
• Place right side down on lining, pin and baste, cut lining generously.
• Sew around bib on sewing line, leave gap for turning at centre front. Use running stitch, with backstitch at corners and changes of direction.

• Remove basting threads, trim to cutting line, clip corners and inside curves, turn right side out. Attach a silk thread to the seam allowances of points, push needle, eye end, inside and out through the turning gap, pull right side out gently. Smooth and press.
• Overcast neck edge neatly closing turning gap.
Work needlelace edge (fig. 17) if you wish.
• Sew bead and embroider loop to close.

PILCHERS

You will need
  Printed or plain lawn, silk habutai for lining, 4 beads

Method
    • Trace and cut pattern for pilchers on straight of grain.
    • Place pilchers right side down onto silk lining, pin and baste.
    Cut lining with a generous margin.
    • Sew around pilchers on sewing line, leave a gap for turning at waist back. Use running stitches and backstitches on corners and changes in direction.
    • Remove basting, trim both fabrics to cutting line, clip inside curves and turn right side out, making sure all corners are crisp. Press.
    • Overcast and slightly gather back waist edge and back leg edges, closing turning gap in passing.
    • Sew 2 beads each side of back and embroider 2 matching loops on each side of front to close.

SUN BONNET

YOU WILL NEED

Printed or plain lawn, silk habutai for lining, 150 mm (6 in) silk ribbon to tie

METHOD
- Trace and cut sun bonnet pattern on straight of grain.
- Place right side down on lining pin and baste. Cut lining generously.
- Sew around sun bonnet on sewing line with running stitch, using backstitch at corners and changes in direction. Leave back neck edge open for turning.
- Remove basting, trim to cutting line, clip inside curves, turn right side out and press.
- Overcast neck edge closed.
- Stitch side and back corners together (leave opening on each side for ventilation).
- Attach ribbon on each side, letting it pass across the top of the bonnet, turn brim back over ribbon and tie under chin!

Now for the more formal stuff ...

The petticoat and bonnet are not too taxing, the gown needs close attention.

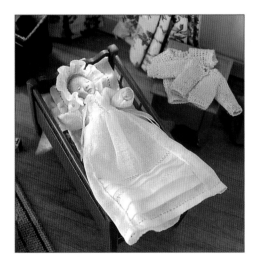

David wearing nineteenth century gown

HALF PETTICOAT

YOU WILL NEED
  Lawn or silk habutai, 200 mm (8 in) shirring elastic

METHOD
  • Cut pattern for petticoat from either silk or lawn on the straight of
  the grain.
  • Fold in ends of waist hem. Fold down and press double fold of waist hem.
  • Place elastic, folded in half, inside fold of hem, loop peeping out one
  end and tails out the other.
  • Hem waist hem over elastic but don't catch the elastic.
  • Make centre back seam with overcasting or run and fell seam.
  • Draw up elastic to fit waist and knot free ends through loop. Trim tails
  and tuck into waist hem.
  • Hem bottom edge with the stitch of your choice. You can make a
  small tuck parallel to the hem if you wish.

TRADITIONAL GOWN

This late nineteenth century design has a central front panel formed by
the bodice front and the skirt front which is the site of the embroidered
enrichment and gives extra fullness to a gown that would otherwise be
very plain and straight. The embroidery and tucks are worked first, then
the bodice front is sewn to the skirt front after the length is corrected by
measuring it against the main part of the gown. Adjust the length from
the top of the skirt. Refer to the diagram showing the construction
sequence before you start.

Traditional gown with bonnet

Construction Sequence for gown (David)

You will need

Silk habutai, lawn or Swiss batiste, silk ribbon for sash, bead

Method

• Trace and cut out pieces for the gown from lawn or batiste on straight of grain. Mark position of tucks and embroidery (indicated on the pattern by the lines of loops) on skirt front and bodice front.

• Cut a facing for the main body of the gown 38 x 70 mm ($1^{1}/_{2}$ x $2^{1}/_{4}$ in) in silk, lawn or batiste as chosen for the gown itself.

• Decide which stitch you wish to use for the embroidery and draw out threads if using hem stitching; 4 should be enough for each line. The short length of embroidery on the bodice front should be done at the same time. Work the embroidered lines on skirt front and bodice front.

• Fold and sew the tucks across the skirt front.

• Position the facing for the main body of the gown from below the back opening shown on the pattern to below the sleeves on the front of the gown, right sides together, pin and baste (see construction sequence).

• Sew around the stitching line including the back opening.

• Remove basting. Clip inside curves and corners, turn right side out and press carefully.

• Fold one side of back opening over the other and stitch in place at the base of opening.

• Measure length of skirt front against front of gown, taking seam allowances into consideration.

• The length of the skirt front when attached to the bodice front should be the same as the length of the gown with a small opening for the neck. If the skirt front is still too long for the gown shorten it from the *top* of the skirt front: there is still a hem to take at the bottom and the tucks need to have space below them for the hem.

• Fold side seam allowances inside bodice front and press. (The unembroidered part of the bodice front is folded back and becomes its facing.)

• Gather the top of the skirt front to fit bodice front.

• Sew skirt front to bodice front then hem bodice front facing to the back of that seam. This forms the front panel of the gown.

• Position the front panel right side over right side of body of gown and overcast both front seams, the folded edge of bodice front to the faced edge of the gown body and the unfinished edges together.

• Tuck in short ends of sleeve hems, fold hem and overcast; gather (fig. 8) the sleeves to fit over baby's hands.

• Fold right side in and overcast side seams.

• Turn up bottom hem and hem with the stitch of your choice. Hemstitching is not suitable here as there are several short lengths to sew.

• Sew bead and embroider loop at back of neck to close.

• Attach ribbon ties to each side of apron front at the base of the bodice; these tie behind.

BONNET

YOU WILL NEED

Silk habutai, lawn or Swiss batiste to match gown, 200 mm (8 in) silk ribbon for ties

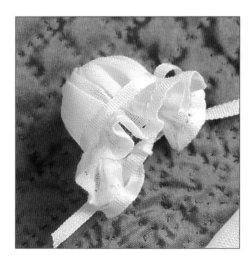

METHOD

- Trace and cut bonnet on the straight of the grain.
- Hem the two short sides of the bonnet with very narrow hems and hem the long hem at the front of the bonnet with the same stitch you used for the bottom of the gown.
- Take a tuck (not shown on pattern as it is optional) 10 mm ($^3/_8$ in) in from remaining edge (back of bonnet) and gather this tightly as you sew, taking backstitches to hold the stitching firmly as you do so: the thread can break if it has to be pulled too tightly for too long. This should end up about 25 mm (1 in) long.
- Gather raw edge with overcast gathering, using a double thread and pulling up as firmly as possible as you go. Join into a circle and sew closed as neatly as you can.
- Gather front of bonnet 7 mm ($^1/_4$ in) from front edge with double thread and occasional backstitches to fit head of baby.
- Sew silk ribbon over front line of gathers. Tie under baby's chin.

ANNABEL

I have to admit to a puritanical streak which can sometimes pull me to a screaming halt when confronted by excess (but not always). A smocked dress for a child is one instance. Smocking with spoke stitch hems, fine; smocking with a Peter Pan collar, fine; smocking with both? No thank you. That is a personal prejudice; you do as you judge best. Sometimes I smock a striped fabric as this can help with the gathers but I tend to avoid other patterned fabrics. Well-executed smocking is a wonderful texture and another pattern in the fabric only adds confusion. Smocking a plain colour with its complementary colour is dramatic. As Annabel is a redhead she wears a lot of aqua and that colour was chosen this time. It is smocked in a deeper shade of that blue-green shade and the collar is edged in that colour too. This dress is made in Swiss batiste. The fabric is delicate so the bodice is lined with the same fabric, slightly intensifying the colour.

Annabel wearing a smocked dress with Peter Pan collar

ANNABEL'S MEASUREMENTS

Height: 105 mm (4^{1}/8 in)

Bust: 60 mm (2^{1}/4 in)

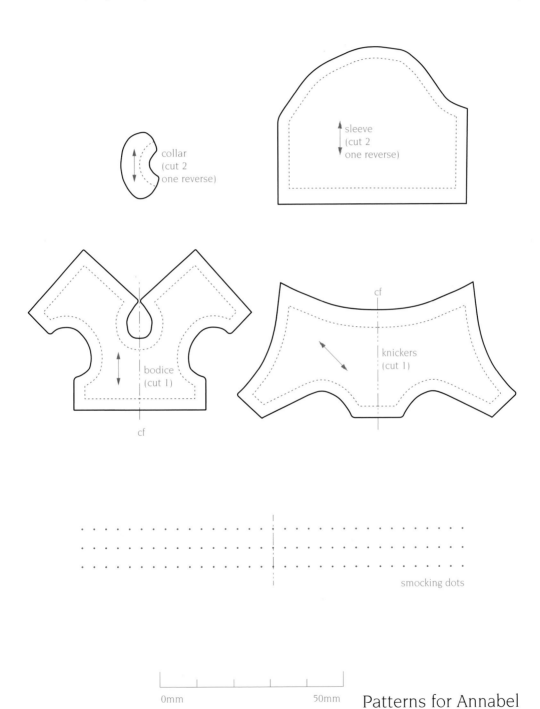

collar
(cut 2
one reverse)

sleeve
(cut 2
one reverse)

bodice
(cut 1)

cf

knickers
(cut 1)

cf

smocking dots

0mm   50mm

Patterns for Annabel

SMOCKED DRESS

You will need

Lawn or batiste for dress, lawn for collar, 2 beads

Method

• Trace and cut dress pieces. Trace collar on contrasting fabric but don't cut out yet. Cut a rectangular piece for the skirt, skirt 210 x 70 mm (8¹/₂ x 2³/₄ in).

• Work the collar first. The pattern dots are on the wrong side of the fabric but the buttonhole edge stitch is worked on the right side. Follow the dots with a line of running stitch: pass needle to the right side and work buttonhole stitch over running stitch.

• Trim the two sides of the collar to edge of buttonhole stitch on the right side, turn and trim neckline on wrong side, don't clip stitching.

• Baste collar pieces to right side of bodice neckline, touching at centre front and leaving a space before centre back on each side. Baste bodice to lining right side down; in this case the lining can be the same fabric as the top. Cut lining with generous margin.

• Sew back, neck and underarm seams through all layers; leave arm-holes and waistline open.

• Trim seam allowances, clip inside neck curve, turn right side out. Press.

• Check left and right sleeves to make sure you have one of each. Turn in short side of sleeve hems, fold up hem, press and hem. If using spoke stitch on the dress this is one other place to use it.

• Gather sleeve above hem to fit elbow with a double thread to match the fabric, then work over the gathering with chain stitch in thread to match the smocking.

• Gather top of sleeves to fit armhole and sew in place with small running stitches. Trim and over cast raw edges.

• Overcast underarm and sleeve seams. Turn right side out. Press.

• Check fit of bodice.

• Mark centre front of skirt in seam allowance at waistline, then divide in half again to find the points matching the side seams on bodice.

• Trace smocking dots on wrong side of fabric, matching centre front marks. Work the three lines of basting (fig. 12). You should use knots this time as the basting is temporary. Draw up gathers to fit bodice front and knot off ends. The smocking is on the front of the dress only.

• Work smocking (fig. 12) using 2 lines of rope formation and 4 or 5 rows of cable formation. Leave basting in place until bodice is attached.

• Sew back seam, either overcasting or a French seam, leaving an opening placket 25 mm (1 in) below waistline. Hem edges of placket with tiny hems and small stitches.

• Gather skirt back to fit bodice back.

• Attach skirt to bodice, matching centre front and side seam marks. Use running and backstitches for this, trim, then overcast raw edges. Press waist seam upwards.

• Double fold and sew hem with the stitch of your choice. Press hem.

• Attach beads and embroider loops at the back of the bodice to close.

KNICKERS

You will need

Silk habutai or lawn, 150 mm (6 in) shirring elastic

Method

• Trace and cut pattern from either silk or lawn with the grain on the bias.

• Fold in ends of waist hem and baste in place (small stitches).

• Fold down and press double fold of waist hem.

• Place elastic, folded in half, inside fold of hem, loop peeping out one end and tails out the other.

• Hem waist hem over elastic but don't catch the elastic.

• Fold and hem leg edges of knickers with tiny hems.

• Turn right side in and overcast or run and fell centre back seam.

• Draw up elastic to fit waist and knot free ends through loop. Trim tails and tuck into waist hem.

• Overcast seam between legs firmly. Turn right side out and press.

LACHLAN

The sailor suit is an all-time classic favourite, of mothers, if not of boys themselves. The blue and white striped fabric could be replaced with red and white stripes or plain white. The collar is a single thickness of fabric with its outer edges bound with silk ribbon.

Lachlan wearing his sailor suit

UNDERPANTS

You will need
Lawn, 200 mm (8 in) shirring elastic

Method
- Trace and cut underpants on the bias.
- Hem leg seams, turning in short ends of hems.
- Overcast one side seam.
- Turn in short ends of waist hem and fold down hem, press.
- Fold elastic in half, tuck inside fold of waist hem with loop of elastic peeping out one end and tails out the other.
- Hem waist hem with elastic inside, but do not catch the elastic.
- Pull up elastic to fit waist, knot free ends through loop, trim ends.
- Overcast remaining side seam, turn right side out and press.

SAILOR SUIT JACKET

You will need
Lawn or suitable fabric for body of jacket, white lawn for collar, striped lawn for insert behind collar, 4 mm ($5/32$ in) ribbon to bind collar to tone or complement body fabric, red ribbon for trim, 2 beads

Method
- Trace and cut pieces for jacket from body fabric and collar from white. Cut outer edge of collar but leave neck edge uncut until outer edge is bound with ribbon.
- Bind collar with ribbon by sewing selvedge of ribbon on the right side of collar with small running stitches. The seam allowance is 2 mm ($1/16$ in). Fold extra ribbon at corners, enough to make a neat mitre when unfolded.
- Fold ribbon over raw edge of collar and hem in place, making corners neatly, press. Cut out neck to 3 mm ($1/8$ in) seam allowance.

LACHLAN'S MEASUREMENTS

Height: 95 mm ($3^3/4$ in)

Chest: 50 mm (2 in)

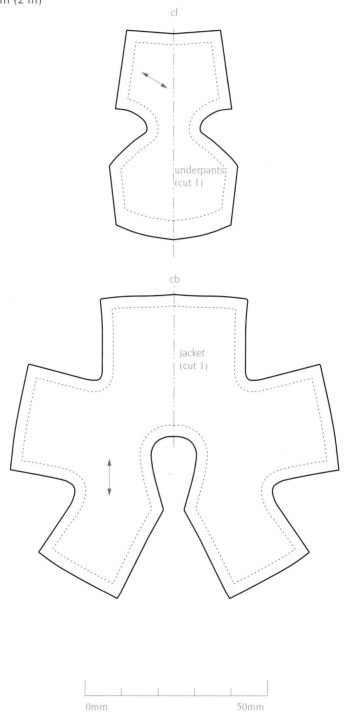

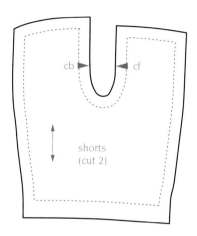

cb ▶ ◀ cf

shorts
(cut 2)

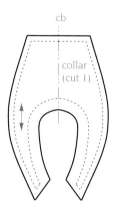

cb

collar
(cut 1)

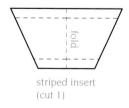

fold

striped insert
(cut 1)

Patterns for Lachlan

- Place collar right side up on right side of jacket, pin and baste in place.
- Place jacket with collar right side down on lining and pin and baste in place.
- Sew all round jacket, through all layers, leaving a small gap for turning in one of the side seams.
- Trim seam allowances, clip inside curves and turn right side out, making sure all corners are crisp. Press jacket and collar.
- Fold right side in and sew underarm and sleeve seams, turn right side out.
- Fold striped insert on foldline, right side in, and sew, turn right side out and press. Attach to inside front of jacket on the right hand side so that it shows behind the sailor collar but tucks underneath.
- Sew on beads and work embroidered loops to close. Attach red ribbon trim to base of collar.

KNEE SHORTS

I made the first pair of these in the navy and white striped fabric, but this was not satisfying visually, so I made another pair in the same fabric as the jacket. This is a simple pattern with elasticised waist. Follow the construction sequence closely, at least for the first time. The seams on the outside leg give the shorts a very satisfactory shape.

You will need
  Fabric for shorts, 200 mm (8 in) shirring elastic

Method
- Trace and cut the patterns from fabric for shorts. Pin and baste right sides together.
- Overcast seam from front waist to back waist (fig. 4).
- Check length of shorts on your figure and fold up hem, turning in short ends of hem at side seams and hem both legs.
- Overcast one side seam. Turn right side out and open out.

- Fold down and press waist hem, turning in short ends of hem in the seam allowances at each end.
- Place elastic, folded in half, in the fold of the waist hem, looped end peeping out one side, tails out the other.
- Hem waist, being careful not to catch the elastic in the stitching.
- Turn right side in and overcast the remaining side seam.
- Pull up elastic to fit waist, knot free ends through loop, trim ends.
- Turn right side out and press with ironing sausages.

ISOBEL

Isobel is on the edge of her teenage years, but has not quite reached the Bolshevik stage; the lull before the storm? Perhaps she is the ideal young person—and there won't be one. Anything is possible in miniature.
She has the jeans which, with automobiles, are the emblem of our age. Her striped top is casual enough to wear with the jeans but change them for the pleated skirt and the top looks quite dressy.

Isobel's striped top takes on a sporty character combined with jeans

STRIPED TOP

This raglan design is one way to use stripes without a shoulder seam.
It is faced with silk. There are arguments about whether stripes should be
matched. I prefer to match them but when you use them it is your choice.

YOU WILL NEED
  Lawn (this one was a Liberty stripe), silk habutai for facing, 2 beads

METHOD
  • Trace and cut pattern pieces in striped fabric if using and silk facing
  fabric.
  • Overcast outside edge of silk facing to stop fraying.
  • Turn in short ends of sleeve hems, turn up and hem sleeve hems.
  • Overcast sleeve seams (fig. 4), turn right side out.
  • Sew sleeves into armholes with running stitch, open carefully and
  press flat. Turn right side out.
  • Place facing over top, matching centre front, right sides together.
  Baste facing in place, then sew back hems, back openings and neck with
  running stitch. Trim seam allowances, clip inside curve around neck and
  press. Catch facing to seam allowances inside to keep it in place.
  • Finish hem, sew beads and embroider loops to close.

JEANS

The jeans are made in a lightweight chambray fabric but it is still thicker
than is desirable. To overcome bulkiness in the hems the raw edges are
overcast before only one fold is used when the jeans are hemmed. The
same
principle applies for the waistband. The pockets can be simulated with
embroidery or made to function.

ISOBEL'S MEASUREMENTS

Height: 125 mm (5 in)

Chest: 65 mm (2$\frac{1}{2}$in)

Inside leg length: 65 mm (2$\frac{1}{2}$ in)

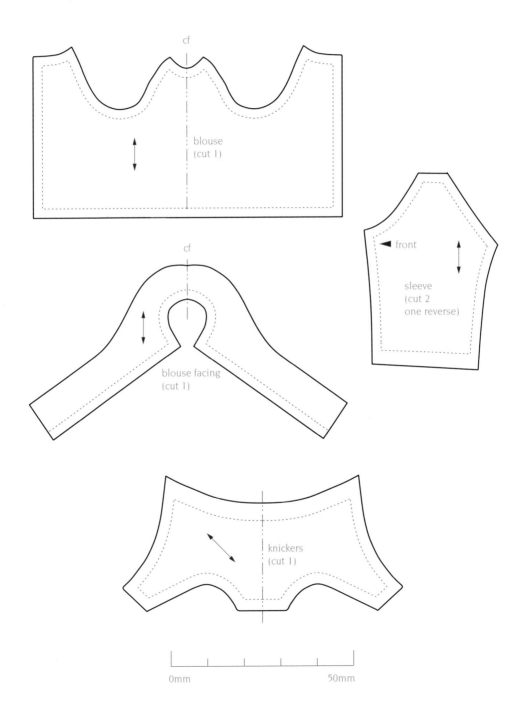

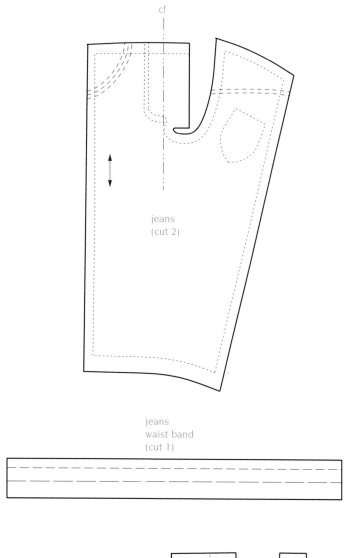

cf

jeans
(cut 2)

jeans
waist band
(cut 1)

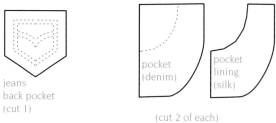

jeans
back pocket
(cut 1)

pocket
(denim)

pocket
lining
(silk)

(cut 2 of each)

Patterns for Isobel

YOU WILL NEED

Chambray or suitable jeans fabric, fine lawn or silk habutai for lining pockets if included, metallic bead

METHOD

• Trace and cut out jeans. If making front pockets functional, cut facing in a fine fabric. The back part of the pocket, the piece you see, should be cut in the same fabric as the jeans.

• Face the front pockets, trim, clip inside curves, turn and press.

• Work contrast stitching on pocket edges in very small backstitch.

• Place the visible back part of pocket lining behind the faced pocket front and sew the pockets together with overcasting from waist to side seam; the rest will be caught in the side seams later.

• Overcast middle seam from below fly opening to back waist.

• Overcast edges of fly opening and turn back right side for girls, left side for boys. Stitch fly to lie correctly.

• Work the contrast stitching fly detail in small backstitches. Then work the stitching details on back yoke and just inside the seam allowances of back side seams. It is very awkward to work those seams' stitching details once the seam is made. The waistband can have the stitching details done in place.

• Turn in short ends of leg hems, turn up and overcast raw edge, then hem.

• Overcast edges of back pocket, work stitching detail, turn in hems and sew allowances to back of detail stitching. Place in position and slip stitch in place.

• Run two gathering threads round waistline to fit waist, ease most fullness to the back.

• Sew waistband in place, folding in front edges, overcast long edge. Fold length of waistband down and hem in place. Backstitch stitching detail on right side.

• Attach metallic bead to waist band and embroider loop to close.

• Use ironing sausages to press.

PLEATED SKIRT

Isobel can wear this skirt with her striped top for less casual occasions. It does up at centre back. The skirt is made from a rectangle of fabric and no pattern is given.

<small>YOU WILL NEED</small>
  Lawn for skirt, bead

<small>METHOD</small>
  A pleated skirt requires a width of fabric 3 times your figure's waist measurement plus another 7 mm ($^1/_4$ in) for seam allowance/placket. Isobel has a hip measurement a little less than 58 mm ($2^1/_4$ in), so the fabric width needs to be 3 times that measurement plus the seam allowance, which is 195 mm ($7^1/_2$ in) wide. (If your figure's hip measurement is different, multiply that measurement by 3 and add the seam allowance.) The depth required for Isobel's skirt happens to be 65 mm ($2^1/_2$ in). (Yours may be different.)

• Cut the skirt on the straight of the grain.
• Isobel's waistband measures 65 x 12 mm ($2^1/_2$ x $^1/_2$ in). The waistband length allows for turnings and overlap. Adjust waistband to fit your figure.
• Turn up skirt along the bottom, turning short ends in, and hem. Press.
• Pleat length of fabric. You could use a pleating device if you have one, but basting, while slower, is more accurate and controllable and you don't need to invest in another piece of equipment. Allowing for seams and placket opening, 195 mm ($7^1/_2$ in) of fabric should reduce to 58 mm ($2^1/_4$ in). Measure off and mark 10 mm ($^3/_8$ in) intervals top and bottom on the wrong side. Fold and baste pleats along the fold between marks (18 or 19 pleats in total). Press pleats in place firmly.
• Sew a line of running stitch along waist edge to draw up to fit the waist of your figure.

• Before removing the basting that holds the pleats, take a thread and secure the back fold of the pleats on the inside one-third of the way down from the waistline. This a permanent line of stitching and should not show on the right side.
• Fold and hem placket 20 mm (³/₄ in) down from waistline on folded side and overcast flat side, which will be overlapped.
• Sew back seam with overcasting so that pleats lie flat on the right side and all raw edges are finished inside.
• Sew waistband to waistline with a combination of running and back-stitches; fold in short ends, then fold and hem remaining edge. Press flat.
• Remove basting. Attach bead and work embroidered loop to close.

KNICKERS

You will need
Silk habutai or lawn, 200 mm (8 in) shirring elastic

Method
• Trace and cut pattern with the grain on the bias.
• Fold in ends of waist hem and baste in place (small stitches).
• Fold down and press double fold of waist hem.
• Place elastic, folded in half, inside fold of hem, loop peeping out one end and tails out the other.
• Hem waist hem over elastic but don't catch the elastic.
• Fold and hem leg edges of knickers with tiny hems.
• Turn right side in and overcast or run and fell centre back seam.
• Draw up elastic to fit waist and knot free ends through loop. Trim tails and tuck into waist hem.
• Overcast seam between legs firmly. Turn right side out and press.

Top right: Isobel in striped top and pleated skirt

ARCHIE

Archie is the adult male, a deliberate portrait of my grandfather so not a token male in any way. His trousers can be made up as jeans using the instructions for Isobel's jeans and making the slight adjustments to the pocket patterns given for hers. If you wish to make the pockets functional, enlarge the curved side slightly. When choosing fabric for the jacket, something like Tana lawn is still the best choice. The fabric needs to be fine because the number of seams can give the garment a very bulky appearance if made in anything coarse. The choice of colour will help the jacket look convincing: this is where clichés and stereotypes come in useful in reinforcing the illusion. If the colour and silhouette are fine the eye is usually satisfied.

Archie wearing a suit

UNDERPANTS

You will need
  Lawn, 200 mm (8 in) shirring elastic

Method
  • Trace and cut underpants on the bias grain of fabric.
  • Hem leg seams, turning in short ends of hems.
  • Overcast one side seam.
  • Turn in short ends of waist hem and fold down hem, press.
  • Fold elastic in half, tuck inside fold of waist hem with loop of elastic
  peeping out one end and tails out the other.
  • Hem waist hem with elastic inside but do not catch the elastic.
  • Pull up elastic to fit waist, knot free ends through loop, trim ends.
  • Overcast remaining side seam. Turn right side out and press.

SHIRT

Check the pattern fit on your figure and adjust as described in the
section on using the patterns.

You will need
  Lawn, 4 metallic beads, beads to match shirt for buttons

Method
  • Trace and cut out all shirt pieces on the straight of the grain.
  • Overcast front edge of inside facings.
  • Sew shoulder seams with running stitch, open flat and press.
  • Fold collar in half along the long fold and sew angled ends, turn
  and press.
  • Fold collar in half to find centre back, match centre back collar with
  centre back of neck and sew to neckline with running stitch. Clip inside
  curves of neckline to fit collar.
  • Fold back front facing, right side in, over collar and sew through all
  layers. Stitch facing at hemline. Turn and press.

ARCHIE'S MEASUREMENTS

Height: 155 mm ($6^{1}/4$ in)

Chest: 85 mm ($3^{1}/4$in)

Inside leg length: 75 mm (3 in)

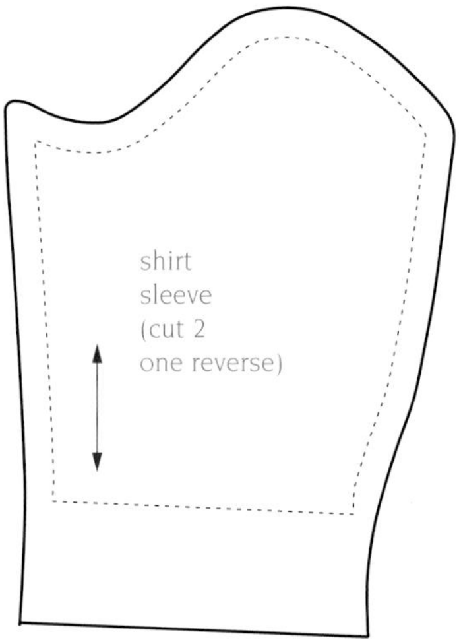

shirt
sleeve
(cut 2
one reverse)

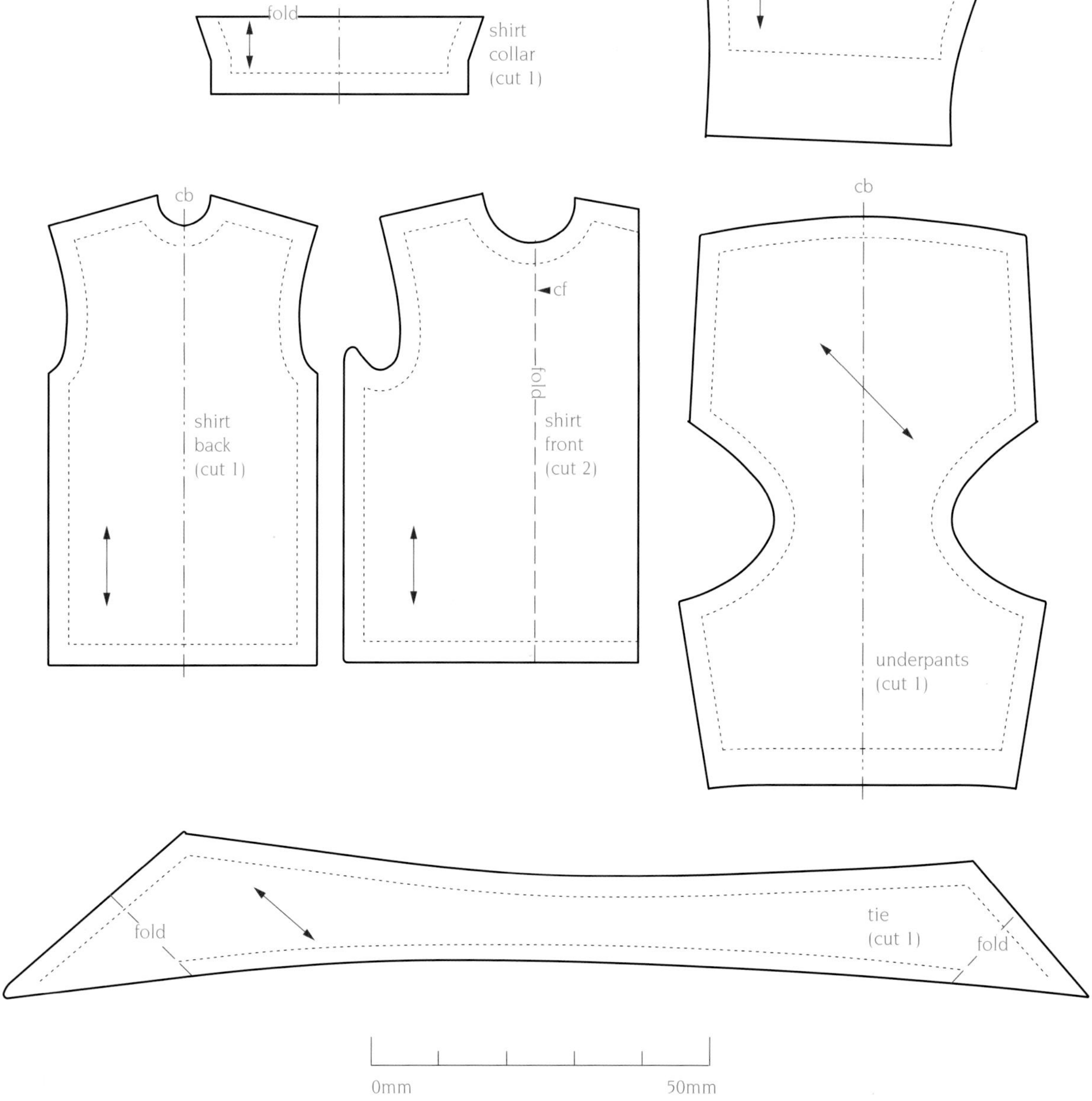

fold

shirt
collar
(cut 1)

cb

shirt
back
(cut 1)

cf

fold

shirt
front
(cut 2)

cb

underpants
(cut 1)

fold

tie
(cut 1)

fold

0mm   50mm

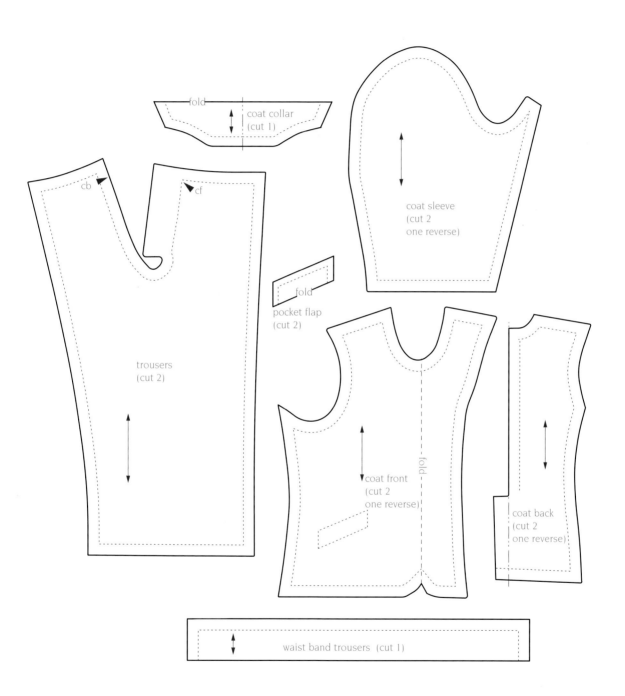

coat collar
(cut 1)

fold

coat sleeve
(cut 2
one reverse)

cb

cf

fold

pocket flap
(cut 2)

trousers
(cut 2)

coat front
(cut 2
one reverse)

fold

coat back
(cut 2
one reverse)

waist band trousers (cut 1)

Patterns for Archie

• Overcast remaining raw edges inside back of neck.

• The seam allowances at the end of the sleeves are turned to the right side to become the shirt cuffs. Remember to allow right and left sleeves. Turn side seam allowances inside the cuffs and overcast each side: these will be left open and closed later with metallic beads to simulate cufflinks. Sew folded hem on right side with small backstitches.

• Run a gathering thread around the top of the sleeves, ease gathers to fit armholes, sew with running stitch, trim seam allowances and overcast raw edges. Press seams towards sleeves.

• Turn right side in, overcast underarm and sleeve seams to cuffs.

• Turn right side out and sew metallic beads on each side of cuffs (check fit on your figure's wrists and that hand can pass through the opening first).

• Hem bottom edge of shirt.

• Mark position of buttons and buttonholes on the fronts of the shirt with tiny pencil dots.

• Sew beads into position on right side of shirt front.

• Work buttonholes in the finest possible thread to match shirt fabric. Make a line of tiny running stitches around mark for buttonhole, carefully cut the hole with your very sharp scissors then closely overcast the edge all round hole.

• Press, using the ironing sausages.

TROUSERS

You will need
Fabric for trousers, lawn or other cotton or matt silk in a suitable colour, bead

Method
• Trace and cut trouser pattern on straight of grain.

• Place two main pieces right sides together and overcast seam from centre back waist to base of fly.

• Overcast edges of fly opening. On left hand side turn fly facing flush with seam and baste in place. Backstitch fly detail on the outside but through both layers. Fold left side of fly over right hand side and stitch in place at the base of fly.

• Check length of trouser legs then fold up and sew hems, turning in short ends of hems at seam allowances.

• Overcast side seams. Turn right side out and press with ironing sausage.

• Measure length of waistband, allow for turning ends in and overlap, trim to correct length.

• Gather back waist of trousers slightly to give a good shape and make a small pleat in each side of trouser fronts to fit waistband.

• Sew waistband in place. Turn in short ends of band, fold length over and hem inside waist, overcast short ends. If the waistband seems bulky, trim second turning fold away with scissors, overcast and then hem in place.

• Attach bead to waistband and embroider loop to close.

JACKET

Check each of these pattern pieces against your figure to see how much adjustment is needed. Don't forget seam allowances will be taken so allow for them. Things like sleeve length can be changed simply; more substantial changes need to use the method described in the chapter on using the patterns. This garment does need proper buttonholes even if you are using beads to close it.

YOU WILL NEED

Fabric for jacket, lawn, silk or a suitably fine fabric to match or contrast with trousers, silk habutai for lining, 3 beads or buttons

METHOD

• Trace patterns onto wrong side of fabric. Cut out sleeves and backs with 7 mm ($^1/_4$ in) margin all round. Cut fronts with the same margin on all sides except front facing which should be cut on the cutting line.

• Cut lining for each front 12 mm ($^1/_2$ in) larger all round than the fronts themselves. Place fronts right side up (check right and left sides), with the facing edges of the fronts overlapping the edges of the lining fabric. This will be sewn in place before the fronts are folded along their front edge and the lining and top fabric are sewn together as usual.

• Pin and baste front facing edges to lining and turn in raw edge and hem to lining with small neat stitches. (These will be seen inside the jacket when it is complete.) Press and remove basting.

• Fold fronts along front edge, right side in. Pin and baste through top and lining.

• Pin and baste remaining pieces to their lining, right sides together. On the back pieces trim left hand flap flush with centre back seam (the other side extends underneath it). The collar piece makes its own lining and is folded inside out and basted.

• Sew around all pieces on the seam lines with firm running stitch, using backstitch where there are corners or a change in direction. Leave armholes, armhole edge of sleeves and a small gap in the back neck of collar open for turning. Remove basting.

• Trim seam allowances, clip inside curves, turn right side out. Make sure all corners are crisp. Press everything.

• Overcast (fig. 5) centre back seam to flap, stitch flap in place. Open and press flat.

• Place fronts and back right sides together and overcast shoulder seams. Press flat.

• Fit collar and overcast, closing opening in back of collar but leaving notches in lapel. Flatten and press into place. Sew collar on from the centre back outwards, right side of collar to inside of jacket (it folds outwards).

• Check fit and adjust again if needed.
Fold down the top of the sleeve lining and baste out of the way to lower part of sleeve so work can be done on the top of the sleeves.

• Run a gathering thread to ease the top of the sleeve so that it fits the armhole. Sew in place through both layers of body and top layer of sleeve with running stitch. Clip underarm seam, remove basting.

• Run a gathering thread along top of sleeve lining. Tuck in raw edge of sleeve lining and hem over raw edges of sleeve seams. Flatten and press with point of iron.

- Overcast side and sleeve seams, easing curved side of sleeve seams into straight side to give elbow fullness. Leave 10 mm (³/₈ in) of sleeve seam open at wrist.
- Turn right side out and press.
- Pocket flaps are decorative and optional, but if you wish to include them, fold in ends, baste, then overcast edges, fold in long edges, press, stitch in place.
- Sew buttons or beads on cuffs, through both sides to close (check hands can still pass through).
- Decide on the number and position of buttons or beads on the front of jacket. This is subject to fashion variations. Mark those and the corresponding positions for buttonholes. Attach buttons and work buttonholes by first doing a line of small running stitches around the hole, clip the slit with very sharp scissors and overcast the raw edges of the hole very closely. Check fit of holes over buttons: stretch slightly if too small, stitch closed if too loose. Breathe a sigh of relief and pat self on back.

TIE

This tie is made on the bias in more or less the proper way. Made in silk habutai, it can be tied in place using the knot of your choice. Each end is self-faced before the long seam is made.

You will need
Silk habutai in a suitable colour

Method
- Trace pattern and cut out tie.
- Fold back triangular ends. One side of point is folded, the other is open. Sew open side on each end. Turn right side out and press.
- Fold in half lengthways, right side in, sew back seam with backstitch and running stitch this gives some stretch. Start at the wide end and finish at the narrow end but *do not cut* thread.
- With thread still attached push eye end of needle back through the tube and out. Gently pull on thread to turn right side out. Cut thread, press and tie.

THE LINEN CUPBOARD

The household in which I grew up inherited my grandmother's Edwardian linen; her damask tablecloths, lace-edged tea cloths and pillowcases, scented with lavender from the garden. I used to open the linen press, breathe that fresh scent and admire. The linen cupboard is a place of fascination in full size: imagine the bliss of beautiful linen for your dolls' house. The techniques that produce clothing in scale can do the same for the linen cupboard. Table mats and napkins, sheets and pillowcases, towels and handtowels are magic in 1:12 scale.

The linen cupboard, showing items of table and bed linen

Choosing the fabric to make the piece is still the first step. Damask is too coarse to use at this scale but plain lawn particularly, or handkerchief linen, if you can find a really fine one, make good table mats and napkins and also sheets and pillowcases. For the tea cloth and napkins with blue embroidery I used a fine cotton batiste; its greater translucency is particularly nice for the greater refinement usually reserved for afternoon tea. (It is still referred to it as 'playing ladies' in our family.) Hemming, hemstitching, spoke stitch and buttonhole stitch are all useful edges for household linen. They can make a plain fabric look elegant. Another elegant touch is a neatly worked monogram in backstitch placed in the corner of a napkin, white on white perhaps, or in a colour to match your decorating scheme. This is one of the places silk embroidery enriches a matt fabric and lends subtle elaboration. It can finish the edge or be used for surface decoration. As these are not stress-bearing situations the fact that thread and fabric are not the same fibre is a less relevant consideration than appearance.

Chair with bathroom items

table mat

tea napkin

dinner napkin

table cloth

hemed table napkin

pillow case top

edge for single sheet

0mm   50mm

Patterns for
linen cupboard

TOWELS

It took some time to decide what was most convincing method for producing bath towels. Loop-textured towelling is almost universal now but that was not always so. I do have some waffle weave towels of contemporary manufacture but waffle weave is not easy to find, or to simulate in 1:12 scale either. Eventually knitting in garter stitch seemed the best solution. The finer the knitting and the thread, the more convincing it is, naturally. Garter stitch also has the advantage of finished edges without the bulk of hems or the perfunctoriness of raw edges. It lies flat without curling the way unrestrained stocking stitch does. The texture is satisfying and it sits well on a rail. As children learning to knit we were set to knit facecloths in a thick cotton yarn so there is some precedence for them in the full scale world. I use No.20 or 21 needles and No.30 cotton thread. If my tension is 10 stitches to 10 mm (25 stitches to the inch) and I want a towel the equivalent of 750 mm (30 inches wide) at 1:12 scale, which is 65 mm ($2^1/_2$ in) wide, then multiply 1 by 65 ($2^1/_2$ by 25 stitches) which gives the result of 65 stitches in all. Work out your tension on the equipment you are using, the size of the item you are making and multiply accordingly. Then keep knitting until it is the right length. Simple. Handtowels and washcloths are made the same way.

Table with dinner mats and napkins

TABLE MATS, NAPKINS, TEA CLOTH

The table mats, napkins and tea cloth with scalloped edges are all made the same way, and use the buttonhole edge (fig. 9). More embroidery can be worked on them if you wish. Trace the patterns on the wrong side of the fabric but don't cut out until the embroidery is complete. Follow the pattern on the wrong side with very fine running stitch, which will give the pattern on the right side without the pencil marks showing. Pass the needle to the right side of the work and work the buttonhole edge and any other embellishment you have decided on. Trim away excess fabric on the right side with small, sharp embroidery scissors, being careful not to cut the stitches. Press. The cloth can be persuaded to drape if necessary by hovering a steam iron over folds made in the right places, but not on the furniture which could sustain damage. Place on the table when completely dry.

SHEETS AND PILLOWCASES

Follow the same procedure as above for the scalloped edges of the sheets and pillowcases. Calculate how long and how wide you need your sheets to be for the bed you are dressing and add extra fabric for working the scalloped edge and the plain hem at the bottom. Make a pattern the size you have calculated and mark your fabric. The long sides can be finished with fine overcasting in a colour to match the fabric; this gives the appearance of a selvedge. Work the scallops following the instructions for the tea cloth. The sheet also has an embroidered line inside the scallops which is worked in backstitch: fold or baste the line to follow. Pillowcases follow the same process but they need to have a second layer on the back. Use the inside backstitch line as the pattern but add seam allowances and a hem allowance on one short side. When the pillowcase top is complete, hem the short side which will remain open and fold back and baste the remaining seam allowances. Hem the basted edges to the back of the backstitches on the pillowcase front to form the case. Don't let the stitches penetrate the top of the pillowcase. Press and place on a pillow.

Table and bed linen can also be made with plain hemmed edges (fig. 3), spoke stitch or hemstitched edges (fig. 11). The embroidery can be worked in a contrasting colour or you can work the buttonhole stitch straight along the edge.

Table with tea cloth and napkins

Bed with bed linen and toys

ACCESSORIES

SHOES

These shoes are made *on* the foot they are for. The foot becomes the last for that shoe so it does fit *that* particular foot. This is one place where glue is the very best thing to use when attaching soles and heels.
The patterns given fit my dolls and may need slight adjustment to fit your figures. Check foot length against the pattern given for the sole in each size. That should indicate if major adjustment is needed. The shoe shapes are simple so should be straightforward to adjust. The shoes are made removable by sewing the back seam with fine overcasting before putting it on the foot *over* the socks or stockings if your figure wears them. Use the finest needle you can handle and #100 silk thread if possible. The outside edge of the shoe upper is eased with overcast gathering around the foot and the sole is glued onto the base of the upper *without gluing the sock or stocking*.

Accessories: hat and shoes

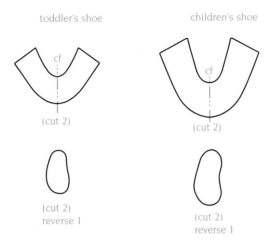

toddler's shoe

cf

(cut 2)

(cut 2)
reverse 1

children's shoe

cf

(cut 2)

(cut 2)
reverse 1

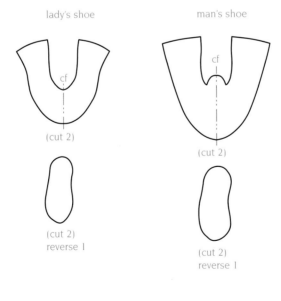

lady's shoe

cf

(cut 2)

(cut 2)
reverse 1

man's shoe

cf

(cut 2)

(cut 2)
reverse 1

0mm   50mm

Patterns for shoes

The best glue to use for this is a good quality PVA. This does take some practice but can be done. Wait until the glue is almost dry before removing the shoe. If you do wish the shoe to come off, it is a good idea to take it off before the glue has set thoroughly to check that none has trespassed onto the sock, otherwise it is impossible to separate the two. Then replace the shoe and allow the glue to dry thoroughly. The hardest thing about making shoes like this is finding the right leather. It needs to be thin, strong enough to sew and hold stitches, flexible and stretchy enough to mould. Old or odd kid gloves are one source. Use proprietary leather dyes to extend the colour range. Joanna and Frances have high heels on their shoes. Their heels are modelled from air-drying clay and covered with the fine leather before being glued in place.

HATS

Hats can be made in a variety of materials—felt, raffia, lace tape, crochet thread. The felt hats are moulded on a head shape. The felt is soaked in PVA glue first to keep its shape when dry. Another technique is what my grandmother used to call a 'hat in hand' technique. This applies to both crochet and sewn tape hats. Start at the centre of the crown, spiralling outwards and shaping the crown as you go. Once it is the size you need, change the angle to make the brim, taper off towards the back when the brim is the size you wish.

I learned about making hats listening to my grandmother tell me stories of her Edwardian youth. This is a process that truly is a 'learning by doing' experience. The result depends on the choice of technique; felt, crochet, straw tape or tape lace, size of the head, the thickness of the braid or thread used; so many variables mean one cannot be specific.

NOTES ON KNITTING

The knitted pieces shown are all things I have designed and made for these dolls. Be warned: there is no way to avoid mathematics in this section and there is lots of counting, multiplying and dividing. It is worth it. Knitting is not my forté but if the hankering is strong enough it is amazing what can be produced. I have always loved Fair Isle knitting: the working of patterns is fascinating and carries the enthusiasm further and there is always that next pattern to see finished. Seeing the pattern grow helps achieve a lot of work with great pleasure. There is also something enchanting about mundane things knitted in miniature. Socks, vests, cardigans and plain baby things all become bright with charm. It is a matter of launching in and experimenting until it works. The patterns vary depending on what thread is available, or most suitable if there is a choice, and the needles. These very fine needles are available from needlework shops that sell miniature needlework supplies and at miniature shows. Again, be warned: while miniature knitting can be addictive, it can also be very hard on hands. Knitting is one of the things that causes my hands to ache if I indulge in too much of the very finest variety. It is the rationing of the time to reduce the pain that makes things take so long to finish. I knit a lot. A moderate amount should cause no trouble.

Knitted garments

Archie wearing a knitted Fair Isle pullover

Remember that maintaining the illusion is the first priority. Some forms of knitting do this better than others. A smooth texture is more successful than a rough one. The stitches seem to relax wider without the pressure of close neighbours. Things like cables and other Arran stitches need to be assessed very carefully. Obviously if a fisherman is being equipped, Arran is the most appropriate. In that case extra fine thread and needles should be employed and if using a dark thread it may well be less frustrating to limit oneself to daylight and times when you are not stressed and tired. Usually stocking stitch and garter stitch are most satisfactory. Fair Isle works if the patterns are reduced as well as the needle size. Keep to the principle of only two colours in a row, although you may use four, five or six colours in all. Draw the patterns on graph paper, one square equivalent to one stitch. Next calculate your knitting tension with the needles and thread you intend using. If doing Fair Isle patterns the result tends to be longer and narrower than your tension would normally give, so allow for that too. Doing a sample is always sensible and here is where the maths comes in. Measure the doll you are knitting for, depending on the garment you require. Work out your tension, the number of stitches to the millimetre (stitches to the inch). Multiply the measurement involved by your number of stitches to the millimetre (stitches per inch). This gives the overall number of stitches. For example, if Archie measures 100 mm (4 in) around the chest, and my tension is 10 stitches to 10 mm (25 stitches to the inch), a total of 100 stitches all around will be required.

Next decide on the design of the garment. If it is to be a cardigan, will you knit the body as three separate pieces or as one piece? If you decide on three pieces, 100 (or the appropriate number for your item) stitches have to be divided between front and back with stitches added for over-lap at the front. Imagine what the shapes look like; how wide does each piece need to be? how long? Make a sketch of the shapes, as accurately as possible. If it is Fair Isle, I map the pattern on graph paper too so that I know how the design fits around the armholes and neck. A cardigan can be a raglan design where the top of the sleeve reaches to the neckline or it could have shoulder seams and armholes. Knitting is accommodating by nature so the shapes are simple.

THREADS

Wool is a wonderful fibre but hard to use in miniature because, to be fine enough for this scale, there are not enough fibres in the thread for strength, at least in the examples I have tried. In a slightly larger scale, 1:8, Medici crewel embroidery wool is lovely and comes in a wonderful range of colours. In 1:12 scale, however, it is very thick and when knitted on very tiny needles the result is stiff and unconvincing. Silk and cotton threads are much more satisfactory to knit. Those shown are usually used for machine and hand sewing. The No.30 cotton thread and Gütermann S303 pure silk thread are my preferred knitting fibres. The silk thread is not very lustrous when knitted and looks convincing at this scale. Mercerised cotton thread can retain its sheen but that can be quite nice anyway. Other cotton threads don't have the lustre and approximate wool quite well. 'Flower' thread (several brands, used for cross stitch embroidery) is very matt but can be rather thick.

KNITTING NEEDLES

There are several ways of designating knitting needle sizes for miniature knitting. The best advice I can offer is to choose what works for you and stick with it, otherwise confusion looms. I use needles in UK sizes 20 to 24. Socks are knitted on either 22 or 24, jumpers and cardigans on 20, 21 or 22, depending on who the garment is for and how thick the thread is. Larger items and thicker thread allow the larger needles.

Sizes of knitting needles tend to vary around the world. Margaret Morgan's guide for knitting needle sizes, given here, is my best information so far.

Metric (mm)	US	UK	Europe
0.5	0000 0000	24	20
0.6	0000 000	24	20
0.75	000 000	22	19
1.0	00000	19/20	18
1.25	0000	18	17
1.5	000	15	15
2.0	0	14	14

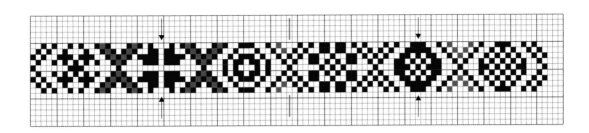

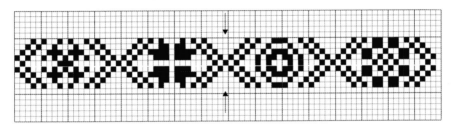

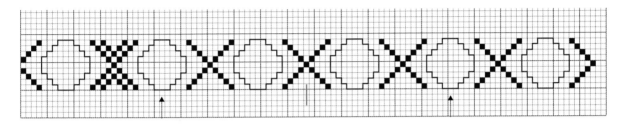

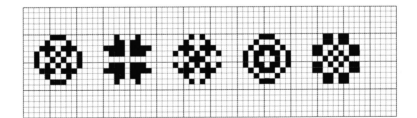

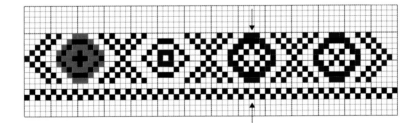

Graph showing Fair Isle patterns

BIBLIOGRAPHY

Bradfield, Nancy 1968, *Costume in Detail*, Harrup, London.

Carrington, James 2000, *Making 1/12 Scale Character Figures*, Guild of Master Craftsman Publications, Lewes, East Sussex.

Don, Sarah 1979, *Fair Isle Knitting*, Mills & Boon Ltd, London.

Eaton, Faith 1994, *The Ultimate Dolls' House Book*, Dorling Kindersley, London.
—1997 (1990), Classic Dolls' Houses, Phoenix, London.
—2002, *Dolls for the Princesses*, The Royal Collection, London.

Gostelow, Mary 1982, *Mary Gostelow's Embroidery Book*, Penguin Books, Middlesex.

Hayden, Ruth 1980, *Mrs Delany: Her Life and Her Flowers*, Colonnade Books, London.

Kamitsis, Lydia 1996, *Vionnet*, Thames & Hudson, London.

McElroy, Roxanne 1997, *That Perfect Stitch*, The Quilt Digest Press, Chicago.

Martin, Richard and Koda, Harold 1993, *Infra-apparel*, The Metropolitan Museum of Art, New York.

Peacock, John 1997, *The 1920s*, Fashion Sourcebooks, Thames & Hudson, London.
—1997, *The 1930s*, Fashion Sourcebooks, Thames & Hudson, London.
—1997, *The 1950s*, Fashion Sourcebooks, Thames & Hudson, London.

Willett, C. and Cunnington, Phillis 1992 (1951), *The History of Underclothes*, Dover Publications, New York.

SUPPLIERS

AUSTRALIA

Fabrics; lace; hat straw
Dollhouse and Craft
PO Box 39, Margate Qld 4019
Ph: 07 3885 9221
www.dollhouseandcraft.com
A catalogue is available.

Needles; thread; lace; knitting needles
Thumbelina
PO Box 242, Henley Beach SA 5022
Ph: 08 8356 3437
Fax: 08 83551008
www.thumbelina.net
A catalogue is available.

Knitting needles; knitting patterns; yarn; buttons
Mini-Mad Mates
Ph: 08 8261 7608 or 08 8298 3480
Email: minimadmates@picknowl.com.au
http://homepages.picknowl.com.au/minimadmates

Knitting needles; knitting patterns; yarns
Alice's Emporium
59 Summerleas Road, Fern Tree Tas 7054
Ph: 03 6239 1182
Email: alice@southcom.com.au

UNITED KINGDOM

Fabric
Liberty of London
www.liberty.co.uk

Fabric; lace; knitting supplies
JLB
80a Crayford High Street, Crayford, Kent DA1 4EF
Ph. 01 322 553325
www.jlbminiatyres.co.uk
A catalogue is available.

Fabric
Willow, HeeBee + Fabrikits
95 Town Lane, Mobberley, Knutsford, WA16 7HH
Ph: #44 (0) 1565 87 22 25 Fax: #44 (0) 1565 87 22 39
Email: care@willowfabrics.com
Web: www.willowfabrics.com
A catalogue is available.

Beads
Ann Crompton
1 Northgate Gardens, Devizes Wilts, SN10 1JY
Ph. 01380 723848

Needles; silk gauze
Miniature Embroideries
Rosedale, Tall Elms Close, Bromley, Kent BR2 0TT

Threads
Pipers Silks
Chinnerys, Egremont Street, Glemsford, Suffolk
CO10 7SA

Threads
Mulberry Silks
Silkwood, 4 Park Close, Tetbury,
Gloustershire GL8 8HS

UNITED STATES OF AMERICA

Decorative buttons; trims
Hestia House
Box 12, Cornwall, CT 06753

Fabric; lace; trim
Sandy's Lace and Trim
7417 North Knoxville, Peoria, IL 61614

GENERAL INFORMATION

International Guild of Miniature Artisans, Ltd
PO Box 629, Freedom, CA 95019
www.igma.org

The Miniature Costumier

ACKNOWLEDGEMENTS

The person whom I would most like to acknowledge for 25 years of friendship, critical appreciation and encouragement, and twelve months of incisive comment (not to mention correcting spelling when the spell checker failed), has specifically forbidden me to do so. She knows who she is and a few others can guess. Thank you.

The photographs are full of the treasures collected for the family in this book. They were created by the following people.

China and porcelain
Dinner service; tea service: Stokesay Ware, 37 Sandbrook Road, Stoke Newington, London, N16 0SH, UK
Vases: Avon Miniatures, 20 Brandize Park, Oakhampton, Devon, EX20 1EQ, UK
Teal vase: Carol Mann, 1 Home Farm, Westhorpe, Southwell, Notts. NG25 0NG, UK

Furniture
Dining table; crib; chairs; chiffonier: Greg Cranwell, 19 Ernest Terrace, Wallaroo SA 5556, Australia
Piano; piano stool; needlework table; Regency couch: David Booth, 16 Narrabeen Road, Cheriton, Folkestone, Kent CT19 4DD, UK
Elbow chair with cane: Nicole Walton Marble, Box 11, Flat Rock, NC, 28731 USA

Glass
Ferenc J. Albert, 449 Capri Court, Marko Island, FL 34145, USA

Hair brushes and personal items
Lawrence and Angela St Leger, 17 Stuart Way, Bridport, Dorset, DT6 4AU UK

Iron; television
Victor Franco, Pinzon #195 - Alamedas, Atizapan, Edo. de Mexico, C.P. 52970, Mexico

Needlework
Carpets; quilts; soft furnishings: Catriona Hall, Australia

Painting
Helen Davies, Australia

Sampler
Margaret Morgan, PO Box 242, Henley Beach SA 5022, Australia

Silver
Mike Sparrow, 16 Stockdale Walk, Knaresborough, N. Yorks. HG5 8DZ, UK

Toys
Helen Davies, Australia and Catriona Hall, Australia

Vacuum cleaner
Kummerows, Box 193 Atascadero, CA 93423, USA